THE
WELL-PLANNED
GARDEN

SUE PHILLIPS

WEIDENFELD AND NICOLSON
LONDON

D1315677

Copyright © George Weidenfeld & Nicolson Ltd 1992

First published in 1988 by
George Weidenfeld & Nicolson Ltd
First published in paperback in 1992 by
George Weidenfeld & Nicolson Ltd
91 Clapham High Street, London SW4 7TA

British Library Cataloguing in Publication Data
A catalogue record for this book is available from
the British Library

Created and produced by Phoebe Phillips Editions

Designers: Rachael Foster, Phil Kay

Illustrators: Lee Travis (main gardens)
Jennifer Abbott
Emma Sharp
Siân Walters

CONTENTS

Introduction   4

Mixed Borders   8
Variation One: Low Maintenance
Variation Two: Shady
Variation Three: For Flower Arrangers
Variation Four: Nutrient-Poor

Herbaceous Beds   26
Variation One: Blue and White
Variation Two: Pink and Silver
Variation Three: For an 18ft × 13ft (5.3m × 4m) Bed
Variation Four: Beside a Wall, Hedge or Fence

Herb Gardens   38
Variation One: Classical
Variation Two: Decorative
Variation Three: Herb Border
Variation Four: Herb Containers

Old-Fashioned Borders   50
Variation One: Scented
Variation Two: Traditional
Variation Three: Border for Cut Flowers
Variation Four: Shady

Paved Gardens   66
Variation One: Purely Perennial
Variation Two: Mainly Evergreen
Variation Three: Introducing Bulbs
Variation Four: With Herbs

Rose Gardens   82
Variation One: With Ground Cover Plants
Variation Two: With Dwarf Shrubs
Variation Three: Fragrant
Variation Four: With Extra Height

Conifer Beds   94
Variation One: Gold
Variation Two: Emphasizing Form
Variation Three: Low-Growing
Variation Four: With Ground Cover

Shrub Borders   104
Variation One: 25ft × 15ft (7.6m × 4.5m) Border
Variation Two: Emphasizing Foliage
Variation Three: Year-Round Colour
Variation Four: Fragrant

Dry, Sunny Beds   118
Variation One: Dry and Shady
Variation Two: Exposed
Variation Three: Island Bed
Variation Four: With Annuals

Summer Borders   132
Variation One: Colour Contrasts
Variation Two: Colour Harmony
Variation Three: Foliage
Variation Four: With Perennials

Water Gardens   144
Variation One: Wildlife Pond
Variation Two: Boggy Banks
Variation Three: Circular Pond
Variation Four: Pond for Fish

Woodland Gardens   160
Variation One: Acid Soil
Variation Two: Alkaline Soil
Variation Three: Damp Soil
Variation Four: Wildflower Garden

Introduction

The Well-Planned Garden contains 60 plans for a variety of gardens ranging from herbaceous borders to conifer beds, rose gardens to woodland clearings.

Once you have chosen the plan you like, it is simply a matter of following individual instructions: *The Well-Planned Garden* shows that you don't have to be a dedicated gardener to have a beautiful garden, in the same way that you don't have to be a chef to follow a recipe. And, just like a cookery book, it is arranged as a series of 'recipes' – for a variety of gardens.

There are twelve self-contained chapters, each consisting of a garden plus four variations. The main 'recipe' starts with a list of ingredients – the plants you will need, season by season, and also exact quantities of materials like garden fertilizer and compost, that you will require for your first year's gardening, plus a list of necessary tools: everything that's needed to create the garden.

The method that follows takes you through the seasons with detailed, step-by-step instructions on how to plant (from the depth of the hole you dig to the kind of dressing you add to the soil), when and exactly how to prune or deadhead the flowers, which plants need supporting, how to cut back and tidy up individual plants when autumn and winter come. . . . Planting instructions are in the tinted column.

The plants used in this 'main recipe' are shown individually at the opening of each chapter linked to the list of ingredients, and impressionistically combined in an illustration of the bed or border at the start of the method. This, in turn, is linked with a planting plan on which coloured areas indicate which plants are in bloom at the height of the flowering season (where relevant – herbs, for example, are not grown primarily for their flowers). This is an ideal: flowering times can vary according to local weather conditions and even the micro-climate in your garden. For correct distances between plants, follow the positioning of the plant numbers on the plan.

In the variations that follow, some or, occasionally, all the plants are replaced to create different effects. These include new colour schemes and shapes, easy care or scented versions, and gardens that are suitable for specific sites – shade or sun.

In the plans that accompany the variations, replacement plants are shown in yellow, with flowering times given in the caption. Maintenance information and quantities (in the variation ingredients) are given for these plants only. Check with the 'main recipe' for instructions on how to tend the remaining (original) plants and how many of them to buy.

Most individual plants are drawn to scale although, in cases where leaf or flower shapes or texture are especially important, a detail is sometimes shown rather than the entire plant. Each plant falls into one of the following height categories, given in its caption:

Dwarf: up to 12 inches (30cm)
Short: from 12 inches (30cm) to 3ft (90cm)
Medium: from 3ft (90cm) to 6ft (1.8m)
Tall: over 6ft (1.8m)

A word about plant names

Latin plant names enable gardeners in all parts of the world to speak a common language, and they are used throughout the book in the lists of ingredients. Names are abbreviated when this is the form in which they are commonly known. Frequently used common names are in brackets in the ingredient lists; these and other, more unusual, ones are given in the index.

Timing operations

Maintenance instructions take you through the gardening year, month by month. Remember, though, that these dates are the ideal and, like flowering times, can be affected by local weather conditions and even your garden's micro-climate.

Be guided by what the plant tells you. When it starts to grow (usually, when it is available from garden centres) is the best time to plant it; the time to cut it back is when it starts to die back naturally. Similarly, if the winter has been a hard one, delay pruning in spring for a few weeks until the weather improves.

Many gardeners prefer to do an entire planting job in one go, and conventional planting times are therefore not always followed in this book: some of the herbs in Herb Gardens could in fact be planted earlier than May; roses are normally planted between November and March when they are dormant, but we occasionally suggest using container-grown specimens and planting them in April with other plants in a plan.

Additional reminders for continuing care are in boxes and start 'In subsequent years. . . .' Other extra information, also in boxes, is headed 'Special note'.

Soil preparation

Preparing soil can be anything from a major to a relatively minor undertaking.

If a site has not been cultivated before, you will need to work material in to improve the soil. This is especially necessary if it is sandy or clay soil, because plants do not generally grow well in these conditions. Peat is often used, but can be expensive if there is a large area to treat. If you live in an area where farmyard or stable manure is available, this can be used provided it is very well rotted. You can also make your own soil improver by composting garden rubbish in a heap or a special compost bin until it resembles good soil.

To dig soil properly, do not just turn over the top layer to the depth of the spade – go deeper. Start by digging out a trench the width of your spade right across the plot. Stack the soil in a heap near the far end of the plot; you'll be needing it later. Use a fork to loosen the soil at the bottom of the trench, then put a layer of peat,

manure or compost in the bottom of it. Now take the spade again and dig a second row to form a new trench alongside the first, using the soil from the new trench to fill in the old one.

As you dig, turn the soil over so it lands in the trench upside down, burying any annual weeds in the process. If you spot any thick white roots, pull them out and throw them into a bucket – the chances are they will be perennial weeds which need to be got rid of. Continue working your way backwards across the plot, digging a new trench and filling in the old one each time. When you have dug your way right across the plot, use the soil from the first trench to fill in the last one.

As an alternative, you can hire a rotovator to do the digging although, in actual fact, using a rotovator is not much less effort than digging in the first place. Unless you have a large and powerful model, you may find that it does not dig deeply but just skims the surface. If you doubt your capabilities, hire an experienced operator to come and do the rotovating for you. He'll know the technique for getting the best out of it.

Ground that has been deeply dug before, and regularly cultivated since, does not need so much effort. Simply spread peat, manure or compost in a layer over the surface – the rate varies slightly according to what you are going to plant, but on average allow 2 × 2 gal (10 litre) bucketfuls per sq yd (sq m). Work backwards across the plot as before and dig so that as the soil from each row is turned over, the compost on top of it is turned under and buried.

When you have finished digging the soil should be roughly level, but it will be covered in large clods. These must be broken up before plants can be put in. To do this, use a rake in long sweeping movements backwards and forwards. The teeth break the lumps into a fine, level tilth, and collect up stones as they go. Stop periodically and gather the largest stone into a bucket, to get rid of them later.

Fertilizer should ideally be spread a few days before you intend to plant the plot. For gardens in this book, I suggest you spread Growmore fertilizer at a rate of 4oz per sq yd (100g per sq m) and rake it in, leaving the soil level. Sprinkle the products at the manufacturer's recommended rate and make sure to get them as evenly spread as possible. If you find it difficult to distribute granules evenly, you'll find it helps to mark the plot out into squares of approximately 1yd (1m) and deal with each one individually. After treating the whole area, rake the soil lightly so the granules are mixed into the surface.

Soil pests killer is also best applied a few days before planting; follow the manufacturer's instructions and rake well in.

On clay soils, incorporate pea grit at the rate of about $1\frac{1}{2} \times 2$ gal (10 litre) bucketfuls per sq yd (sq m), as well as peat, compost or manure, if you are working with herbaceous plants: their roots remain in the ground over winter and can easily rot in heavy clay soil.

When growing plants that are specifically acid or alkali loving, it is a good idea to check the pH factor of your soil. Small soil test kits are inexpensive and easily available from garden centres. To collect a good soil sample, take a trowel and plastic bag and dig a series of holes to the full depth of the trowel, all over the area to be planted. Scoop a small sample of soil from the bottom of each hole and mix all the samples together in the plastic bag. Remove a small quantity to test.

The pH scale runs from 0 to 14 and measures how acid or alkaline the soil is (0 is acid, 14 alkaline).

After planting

When you have finished planting it is advisable to spread a thin layer of peat or well-rotted garden compost or manure between the plants. Mulching, as this is called, has many beneficial effects; it smothers weed seedlings, improves the soil by adding organic matter to it, insulates the roots of the plants from heat in summer and cold in winter and helps to retain moisture in the soil (particularly important in the case of annuals, which are very shallow-rooted). It also provides a pleasingly uniform dark background to the plants. Mulch again every spring as the growing season begins.

Watering

When your garden is newly planted, you must make sure that your plants receive sufficient watering. This is particularly important in the case of bedding plants which, being shallow-rooted, are very vulnerable to the top layer of soil drying out. After about a month, when the roots have penetrated deeper into the soil, looking at its surface is no longer enough. You need to either stick your finger or the probe of an electronic meter into the soil to a depth of 3–4 inches (7.5–10cm). If you are still unsure, dig out a handful of soil to the depth of the trowel and inspect it for moisture.

Weeding

Perennial garden weeds like couch grass, nettles, thistles and docks can be eradicated either by chemicals or by hand. For the chemical method, use a very safe herbicide called Glyphosate which is best applied in spring. This can be watered on with a can or sprayed, and after the weeds are dead the soil can safely be replanted straight away.

By hand, results are slower as, after the weeds have been dug out, fragments of root often remain so that the weeds regrow. This is particularly true with couch grass, where digging up is akin to a form of propagation.

To save yourself quite a bit of work, just dig in annual garden weeds like groundsel, chickweed etc. Being annual, they will not regrow from the roots. It is however a good idea to run a hoe over the ground after digging, as displaced plants may simply re-root if they are not properly covered with soil.

Pests and diseases

These are the bane of every gardener's life and the first rule is: know your enemy. Accordingly, here is a list of the most common problems you can expect to affect the planting schemes in this book.

Aphids Also known as greenfly, blackfly and blight, these pests feed on plant sap, thus distorting young growth. They also leave behind them a sticky dew which attracts black mould. They are round-bodied insects which may be green, brown, cream or pink and they are particularly fond of roses, where they can be found clustering on the growing stems and buds. Spray them with nicotine, malathion, pirimicarb or a systemic insecticide such as dimethoate.

Blackspot This is a rose disease which generally appears in late spring, manifesting itself as black spots on the leaves. Remove and burn the affected leaves and spray every two weeks with a rose fungicide. Apply a foliar feed, as the disease is worse on weak, unhealthy plants.

Mildew This looks like a dusting of talcum powder which appears in small patches and then spreads, distorting the plant. It is particularly prevalent in cool, humid weather – keep a watch for it in poor summers and in early autumn. Spray with Benlate or copper fungicide.

Pesticides

There are two different kinds of pesticide – contact and systemic. Contact sprays are applied direct to the insects, whereas systemic insecticides are absorbed into the plant, subsequently killing the insects which feed upon it. Systemic insecticides cannot be washed off by rain and do not harm ladybirds, bees or butterflies.

Chemical sprays are highly toxic, so always follow the manufacturer's instructions to the letter. Never mix them unless instructed to do so; dispose of any surplus and wash out the sprayer thoroughly.

Pruning

This is a subject that can cause much anguish among novice gardeners. Instructions are given for the individual plants in this book but as a general rule the main purpose of pruning is to maintain a good shape and to remove any weak or dead shoots. To check whether a shoot is dead or not, look at the inside of it. If it is dead it will be a dull brown colour, while a live, healthy shoot will be a green or creamy colour inside. When you are removing dead shoots, cut back cleanly to just above a live bud so that there is no dead wood left to encourage further die-back.

Special notes

• Unless otherwise stated in the instructions, always use secateurs for pruning and trimming.

• Replacement and additional plants are given at the start of each variation. For quantities of 'original' plants, check with the list at the start of the main plan.

Mixed Borders

They don't look contrived, but the best mixed borders are carefully planned. Here an average-sized bed has been landscaped to provide maximum variety and continuity of flowering. Although roses are normally planted in March, it makes sense, in this case, to buy container-grown plants and put them in at the same time as the others in the border.

This planting scheme needs a reasonably sunny but slightly sheltered site. The bed should have a wall or fence along the back, but you could put up a series of posts and wires, trellis or plastic-coated wire netting for the rose to grow on.

Ingredients for a border 15ft × 4ft (4.5m × 1.2m)

April

12 *Lathyrus odoratus* (sweet peas)

5 *Digitalis purpurea* 'Excelsior' (foxglove)

2 *Astilbe* 'Fanal'

3 *Delphinium* 'Pacific Hybrids'

1 floribunda rose 'Elizabeth of Glamis'

5 *Lilium regale* (lily)

3 *Aquilegia* 'McKana Hybrids' (columbine)

2 *Hosta sieboldiana* 'Elegans'

1 *Senecio laxifolius*

1 climbing rose 'Elegance'

2 *Armeria maritima*

8 *Antirrhinum* 'Floral Carpet'

3 *Dianthus* 'Doris'

May

12 *Lobelia erinus* 'Mrs Clibran'

9 *Nicotiana alata* 'Sensation Mixed'

5 *Petunia* 'Resisto Mixed'

5 *Tagetes patula*

From the garden shed

Small packet of slug pellets

12 × 8ft (2.4m) high brushwood sticks

3 × 7ft (2m) high plant stakes

Plant ties

Weedkiller (optional)

20 × 2 gal (10 litre) bucketfuls of peat, or well-rotted garden compost or manure

Additional peat, etc (optional)

Tools required

Spade

Fork

Rake

Garden line

Hand trowel

Watering can or hose

Secateurs

Edging shears

Hoe (optional)

SENECIO (short)

CLIMBING ROSE
(short)

ASTILBE (short)

AQUILEGIA (short)

DIGITALIS
(medium)

DIANTHUS (short)

DELPHINIUM (medium)

FLORIBUNDA
ROSE (short)

LOBELIA (dwarf)

LATHYRUS (tall)

HOSTA (short)

TAGETES (dwarf)

ARMERIA (dwarf)

NICOTIANA (short)

PETUNIA (dwarf)

ANTIRRHINUM (short)

LILIUM (medium)

Method

Before buying your plants, prepare the ground and have everything ready. Start by marking out the bed with the garden line. Cut alongside the line with the spade to form the boundary of the border. Use the spade the wrong way round so the blade goes into the soil at right angles – this gives you a nice clean edge to the grass in front of the bed which can easily be kept tidy with edging shears later. Remove the line and prepare the soil, applying the peat, manure or compost at the rate of 2 bucketfuls per sq yd (sq m) of bed (see introduction).

April

Before planting Water the roses, sweet peas, foxgloves, astilbe, delphiniums, columbines, hosta, senecio, armeria, antirrhinum and dianthus 12 hours before you intend to plant them.

Prune the roses. Use sharp secateurs to cut back the stems of the floribunda rose, Elizabeth of Glamis, to approximately 6 inches (15cm) above the top of the pot. Cut the strongest stems of the climber down to 12 inches (30cm) above the top of the pot, and cut the weaker stems to 4 inches (10cm). Always cut just above the place where a leaf joins the stem.

Planting Set the roses, foxgloves, astilbe, delphiniums, hosta, columbines, senecio, armeria and dianthus out on the bed, still in their pots, in their planting positions. Turn them so that their best side faces the front of the bed.

Plant from the back of the bed towards the front. This way you are less likely to tread on any plants and, most importantly, it gives you the chance to scuff over footmarks with the trowel.

Lift each pot in turn and mark its exact position with the trowel. Dig a small hole the same depth as the pot in the position you have marked, then knock the plants out of their pots. They will come out quite easily if you tap the base of the pots with the trowel first. If they are growing in polythene containers, these should be cut away carefully without disturbing the ball of roots inside.

MAINTENANCE

Scatter slug pellets evenly over the bed to protect plants from being eaten.

Water whenever necessary, starting the day after planting. Check to see if it is needed by looking at the surface of the soil. If it has dried out, then water again. Do this regularly every few days in dry weather and about once a week if there is some natural rainfall.

Continue watering like this for the first two or three weeks until you can see the plants growing. This indicates that they are becoming established.

In subsequent years, in **March**, prune the roses. Use sharp secateurs and cut any dead or very thin, weak shoots out entirely, right back to the base. Then cut all the stems of the floribunda rose, Elizabeth of Glamis, down to 8 inches (20cm). To prune the climbing rose, cut back the short shoots that carried last year's flowers to within a few inches of the main stem they are growing from. Always cut just above a leaf joint.

As the climbing rose grows bigger, train in new branches to extend the basic framework until the space allocated for the plant is finally filled, with branches spaced evenly over the area. From then on, you will be able to select the best of the new branches to replace some of the older ones. The latter are recognizable by their dark-coloured bark, whereas young shoots have lighter brown or greeny skin. Simply cut out the old branch completely to a convenient junction with another stem and tie the new branch in its place.

Above Mixed border.   **Below** Plan for the border.   Coloured areas indicate flowers in bloom in midsummer. Average flowering periods are listed below:

1 *Sweet peas*: June–September   **2** *Lobelia*: May–September
3 *Nicotiana*: June–September   **4** *Foxgloves*: June–July
5 *Astilbe*: June–August   **6** *Petunias*: June–September
7 *Delphiniums*: June–July   **8** *Floribunda rose*: June–July, September–October   **9** *Tagetes*: June–September
10 *Hostas*: July–August   **11** *Lilies*: July   **12** *Senecio*: June–July   **13** *Climbing rose*: June–October   **14** *Antirrhinums*: May–July   **15** *Armeria*: May–July   **16** *Dianthus*: June–July, sometimes September   **17** *Columbine*: May–June

(**April**)

Taking great care not to break up the rootball, place the plant into its hole. Check that the top of the rootball is level with the surrounding soil, as it is important not to put it any deeper than the plant was growing in its pot. If it is not level, add or remove some soil from the bottom of the hole until it is right.

Make sure the best side of the plant is still facing the front, and give it a slight turn if not. Fill in round the roots with soil. Very lightly firm round the plant with the trowel handle.

The sweet peas and antirrhinums will be supplied growing in trays or 'strips'. Thin or flimsy trays can be torn away, but rigid ones are best removed by giving the base a couple of sharp taps on a concrete path, and then tipping the contents gently out. You will find the roots have grown together into a tangled mass. Separate the individual plants by tearing the compost apart so that each of the plants is left with an approximately equal-sized rootball. Lay these plants in their planting positions.

To plant them, lift each one and mark its position with the trowel as before. Dig a hole wide enough to take the ball of roots, but about 1 inch (2.5cm) deeper. Plant as before, but this time ensure that the rootball is buried slightly below the soil surface – about 1 inch (2.5cm), no more. This is to give the plant a little support and help it to keep upright.

To plant the lily bulbs, dig a hole 9 inches (23cm) deep for each bulb. Set the bulb at the bottom of the hole, with the pointed end up, and press it gently into the soil. Fill in the hole.

Water the plants in. This is to settle the soil round the roots, as well as to help them start growing. Give each of the roses ½ gal (2 litres) of water, other plants 1 pint (500ml) of water each.

In subsequent years, fork over the ground each spring, using the points of the fork to loosen the soil lightly rather than actually turn it over as this would disturb shallow-rooted plants.

Apply fertilizer evenly over the surface of the bed. Growmore can be used at 2oz (50g) per sq yd, or alternatively buy any good general fertilizer and follow the instructions on the packet. Hoe the feed in after scattering the granules and give the bed a thorough soaking with the hose if the soil is dry.

Divide up hosta and astilbe when the clumps become large and overcrowded. The easiest way to do this is to dig them out of the ground, stick two garden forks into the middle of the clump, back to back, and lever them apart. If the pieces are still rather large, repeat the operation. Replant the pieces with lots of young shoots from the outside of the original clump.

Mulch the entire bed each year for weed control and to minimize watering. If, however, you prefer to use another method of weed control you should still mulch around the hosta, astilbe and lilies as they need extra moisture round their roots to grow well. Spread a thin layer of peat or well-rotted garden compost or manure in a 12 inch (30cm) circle round each plant. Water well before mulching if the ground is at all dry, and take care not to break off any of the young shoots.

Scatter slug pellets around new plants and hostas to protect them from damage.

Special note

When you have finished planting it is advisable to spread a thin layer of peat or well-rotted garden compost or manure between the plants. Mulching, as this is called, has many beneficial effects; it smothers weed seedlings, improves the soil by adding organic matter to it, insulates the roots of the plants from heat in summer and cold in winter and helps to retain moisture in the soil (particularly important in the case of annuals, which are very shallow-rooted). It also provides a pleasingly uniform dark background to the plants. Mulch again every spring as the growing season begins.

> **In subsequent years**, in **April**, plant new foxglove, antirrhinum and sweet pea plants every year.

May

Plant the nicotiana, lobelia, petunia and tagetes after all danger of frost has passed, following the same method as for sweet peas and antirrhinums.

> **In subsequent years**, plant new tagetes, petunia, nicotiana and lobelia each year. Water them well in.

Support sweet pea plants by pushing brushwood sticks in amongst them. They may need a little encouragement to start climbing, but once they do they will manage without further help as their tendrils cling to the sticks.

Apply slug pellets every 2–3 weeks, as they dissolve a little every time they get wet. In a rainy summer or when you are watering frequently you will need to be very thorough about renewing them, as slugs are particularly prevalent then.

Continue to water frequently in dry weather.

> **In subsequent years**, scatter slug pellets regularly round new plants as well as round the hostas.
>
> Repeat the cycle of weeding, watering and deadheading as previously.

June

Deadhead regularly. Go over the bed once a week snipping off the dead flowers as close to the head as possible with sharp scissors or secateurs.

Cut columbine flower stems down to ground level, after they have flowered.

When deadheading roses, cut the old flower heads off a short way down the stem, just above a healthy, full-sized leaf. A new shoot will then grow from a tiny bud in the angle where the leaf joins the stem, and it is from this that the next flush of flowers will come.

Weed the bed every two weeks to keep it tidy. If you prefer to use a hoe, be very careful – all the plants in the bed except the roses have very soft stems and are easily cut into or broken right off by careless hoeing. Alternatively, use a weedkiller especially designed for use among annual flowers – this works by preventing seeds from germinating.

Do take great care not to exceed the stated dose, or you can inhibit the growth of your plants too.

If you prefer to keep weeds down by mulching, spread a thin layer of peat or well-rotted garden compost or manure all over the surface of the bed between the plants. This will smother weed seedlings as soon as they germinate,

(June)

Special note

It is particularly important to deadhead sweet peas and tagetes frequently to encourage them to keep producing lots of new flowers instead of setting seed. It is also a good idea to cut sweet peas regularly for the house, as this acts in the same way as deadheading.

but you do have to start with weed-free ground, so hoe before mulching. It will also help the soil to retain moisture, provided you water the soil thoroughly beforehand.

Trim the grass round the edge of the bed if it is set in a lawn. Each time you mow the grass, cut neatly round the edge of the border with edging shears to give a clean finish.

Spray the roses with systemic insecticide against aphids (greenfly) whenever necessary. Examine the plants every week or two to see if they have become infested with these insects, which are very common. They will usually be found in groups living on young shoots, flower buds and the undersides of young leaves towards the top of the plant. Despite their common name, greenfly may also be brown, cream or even pink.

It is also advisable to spray roses regularly against blackspot, another common problem. This is a fungal disease which produces characteristic black spotty marks on the foliage. If you want to keep your plants free of this you will need to spray them with a special rose fungicide every two weeks (or as directed in the manufacturer's instructions).

Train the climbing rose over the wall or fence at the back of the border or, alternatively, over the netting, wires or trellis you have put up especially for it. The idea is to encourage its stems to grow out and form a framework that roughly covers the area you want it to fill. Once this basic framework of branches has been established it is very easy to keep the plant properly organized. Tie the branches in place with plant ties to form what will eventually become this permanent framework.

July

Deadhead the delphiniums late in the month, when the flowers are over. Cut the dead heads off partway down the stem, just above a healthy-looking leaf. In this way you can sometimes coax the plants to produce a few more flowers. After you finish, remove the dead flower heads from the bed. Cut out the central flowering spike of digitalis, after flowering, to encourage flowering side shoots to increase in size.

You may wish to remove the flowers of senecio, as the shrub is grown for its grey felty leaves which set off the flowers around it.

Continue with the jobs described above: watering, providing protection against slugs, weeding, trimming the edge of the border, and spraying and training the roses.

August

Continue watering if necessary (or applying slug pellets in wet weather), weeding, trimming, and spraying and training the roses.

September

Deadhead the floribunda rose, which in a good summer will be producing a second flush of flowers now.

Spray the roses against mildew. This disease is easy to recognize – it looks as if someone has dusted talcum powder over the leaves, stems and flower buds. As it gets worse large areas of the plant may be covered and some of the leaves may even be shed. Mildew can often be a problem in autumn when the weather is dull, cool and humid. Spray with the same general rose fungicide you used in summer to prevent blackspot. Repeat every two weeks.

Towards the end of the month, cut down and remove the dead flower stems and foliage from the lilies when they start to die back naturally. Cut down the flower stems and leaves of the delphiniums, hostas, columbines and astilbes to ground level after they have finished flowering and the leaves start to turn yellow.

Pull out sweet peas, tagetes, petunia, nicotiana and lobelia after all their flowers are finished. Clear any weeds, plant stakes, pea sticks and other debris from the bed.

In subsequent years, prune senecio by cutting out any damaged or straggly shoots. Cut the flower stems back to just above a convenient leaf if you allowed the plant to flower. Armeria and dianthus may need light pruning: select straggly or broken shoots and cut right back to base.

October

Give the floribunda rose a light pruning. All that is necessary is to shorten the stems by about half. This removes most of the leafy growth that would otherwise get blown about by the wind or broken by snow during the winter. Remove the prunings, give the bed a final weeding and leave it tidy ready for winter. Spray the roses against mildew every two weeks. Cut digitalis to ground level.

Pull out antirrhinums after the flowers are over – although they are actually perennial they are best treated as annuals.

Low Maintenance

A traditional mixed border, like the one in the main plan, calls for a certain amount of work. You can, however, have a mixed border without needing to prune roses, train climbers and replace annuals every year, simply by changing these plants for low-maintenance substitutes. This variation is a mixed border that creates a similar visual effect, but needs very much less work.

April

2 *Sedum* × 'Autumn Joy' (replace *Lathyrus odoratus*)

1 *Ruta graveolens* (replaces *Lobelia erinus* 'Mrs Clibran')

4 *Lupinus* 'Russell Hybrids' (replace *Nicotiana alata* 'Sensation Mixed')

3 *Nepeta* × *faassenii* (replace *Tagetes patula*)

3 *Ajuga reptans* 'Atropurpurea' (replace *Petunia* 'Resisto Mixed')

1 shrub rose 'Paul Crampel' (replaces 'Elizabeth of Glamis')

1 *Lonicera periclymenum* 'Serotina' (honeysuckle) (replaces 'Elegance')

3 *Alchemilla mollis* (replace *Armeria maritima* and *Antirrhinum* 'Floral Carpet')

From the garden shed

8 × 2 ft (76cm) high brushwood sticks, if you live in a windy area

SHRUB ROSE (short)

LUPINUS (short)

LONICERA (medium)

RUTA (short)

NEPETA (short)

AJUGA (dwarf)

ALCHEMILLA (short)

SEDUM (short)

April Prepare the bed and plant, following the method described on page 10. The rose needs no pruning before planting except to cut out any dead or very weak shoots.

> **In subsequent years**, snap off the old flower stems of sedum when growth begins. Trim ruta back to old (dark) wood to preserve its bushy shape.

May Push brushwood sticks in either side of each lupin plant for support if you live in a windy area.

Encourage the honeysuckle to start clumbing up on to its supports. Secure the stems in place initially with a few plant ties. Once it has started to climb it will need no further help, as it twines round its supports to hold itself in place.

June Deadhead the shrub rose regularly, as this will encourage it to continue flowering and produce a second flush of flower later in the year. Do not bother removing the flowering stems of senecio, as the flowers form part of this planting scheme.

July Remove the dead heads from ajuga after flowering by clipping lightly with shears.

Deadhead lupins when the flowers are over. Cut the dead heads off partway down the stem, just above a healthy-looking leaf. You may sometimes coax the plants to produce a few more flowers.

September Cut down and remove the dead stems and the foliage of nepeta and lupins after flowering, and the stems and old foliage of alchemilla. Leave the new foliage in the centre of the plants. Remove dead flowers from ruta.

> **In subsequent years**, in **October**, prune honeysuckle only if the plant becomes too big. Simply remove any shoots that are straggly or starting to grow where they are not wanted. Cut just above the place where a leaf joins a stem. Leave dead sedum stems on plants.
>
> The rose does not require regular pruning, but cut out any dead, damaged or overcrowded shoots.

1 *Sedum*: September–October
2 *Ruta*: June–July
3 *Lupins*: May–July
4 *Nepeta*: May–September
5 *Ajuga*: June–July
6 *Shrub rose*: June–July, September–October
7 *Honeysuckle*: July–October
8 *Alchemilla*: June–August
9 *Astilbe* 10 *Foxgloves*
11 *Delphiniums* 12 *Lilies*
13 *Hostas* 14 *Senecio*
15 *Dianthus* 16 *Columbine*

Shady

Most garden plants prefer reasonably sunny locations, but if you have a shady area, opt for this variation which uses shade-loving plants. You will not need any brushwood sticks.

April

3 *Helleborus foetidus* (replace *Lathyrus odoratus* 'Spencer Hybrids')

1 *Euonymus fortunei* 'Emerald 'n' Gold' (replaces *Lobelia erinus* 'Mrs Clibran')

3 *Aruncus sylvester* (replace *Nicotiana alata* 'Sensation Mixed')

3 *Hosta fortunei* 'Albopicta' (replace *Petunia* 'Resisto Mixed')

3 *Ligularia przewalskii* (replace *Delphinium* Pacific Hybrids)

1 *Sambucus racemosa* 'Plumosa Aurea' (replaces 'Elizabeth of Glamis')

3 *Polygonatum multiflorum* (replace *Lilium regale*)

1 *Mahonia aquifolium* (replaces *Senecio laxifolius*)

1 *Lonicera periclymenum* 'Serotina' (honeysuckle) (replaces 'Elegance')

3 *Ajuga reptans* 'Atropurpurea' (replace *Armeria maritima* and *Antirrhinum* 'Floral Carpet')

3 *Alchemilla mollis* (replace *Tagetes patula*)

4 *Bergenia* 'Ballawley Hybrid' (replace *Dianthus* 'Doris')

HELLEBORUS (short)

EUONYMUS (short)

HOSTA (short)

SAMBUCUS (tall)

ARUNCUS (medium)

LIGULARIA (medium)

April Prepare and plant the bed as previously described on page 10.

POLYGONATUM
(short)

MAHONIA (medium)

ALCHEMILLA
(short)

LONICERA
(medium)

BERGENIA (short)

AJUGA (dwarf)

1 *Helleborus*: March–May
2 *Euonymus*: May–June
3 *Aruncus*: June
4 *Hosta fortunei*: July
5 *Ligularia*: July–August
6 *Sambucus*
7 *Polygonatum*: June
8 *Mahonia*: March–April
9 *Honeysuckle*: July–October
10 *Ajuga*: June–July
11 *Alchemilla*: June–August
12 *Bergenia*: April–May
13 *Foxgloves*   14 *Hosta sieboldii*
15 *Astilbe*   16 *Columbine*

June Deadhead bergenia and helleborus by removing the dead flower spikes when all the flowers are finished. Cut the stems down almost to ground level. Do not remove dead flowerheads from mahonia.

July Deadhead aruncus, as above, and cut the stems down.

August Clip the dead heads off ajuga with shears.

September Cut the dead flower stems and the old leaves from alchemilla, but leave the new foliage growing in the centre of the plants intact. Remove the dead flower spikes from ligularia, and cut the stems down almost to ground level.

In subsequent years, in **March**, dig up and divide polygonatum when clumps become too large, as described below (April).

In **April**, dig up and divide bergenia, ligularia, alchemilla, hosta and ajuga plants when the clumps get too big. Use two garden forks back to back to prise the clump apart, and replant only the best pieces with lots of young growth from round the outside of the original clump. Do not, however, treat helleborus this way as the plants dislike disturbance. When mahonia plants get big, cut a few of the oldest branches to ground level.

In **September**, euonymus may require light pruning – cut entire shoots back to a main branch.

Do not cut bergenia down as it is evergreen, but do remove any leaves that are yellow or dried out.

In **October**, prune honeysuckle when the plant gets too big by cutting short any straggly or over-long shoots. Cut to just above a leaf joint.

Sambucus is unlikely to require any pruning as this variety is very slow growing, but cut off any dead or broken shoots as soon as they are seen.

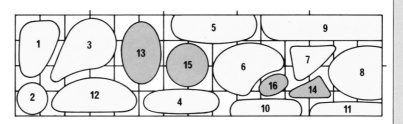

For Flower Arrangers

If you like using flowers indoors, this variation will keep you supplied with something to cut for most of the summer and still leave the garden looking well stocked! Buy the following plants to replace the ones in brackets.

April

1 *Anaphalis triplinervis* (replaces *Lobelia erinus* 'Mrs Clibran')

5 *Achillea* 'Galaxy Hybrids' (replace *Digitalis purpurea* 'Excelsior')

3 *Hosta fortunei* 'Albopicta' (replace *Petunia* 'Resisto Mixed')

1 *Gypsophila paniculata* 'Bristol Fairy' (replaces *Senecio laxifolius*)

3 *Alchemilla mollis* (replace *Armeria maritima* and *Antirrhinum* 'Floral Carpet')

2 *Astrantia maxima* (replace *Tagetes patula*)

May

9 *Nicotiana alata* 'Lime Green' (replace *Nicotiana alata* 'Sensation Mixed')

From the garden shed

12 twiggy brushwood sticks

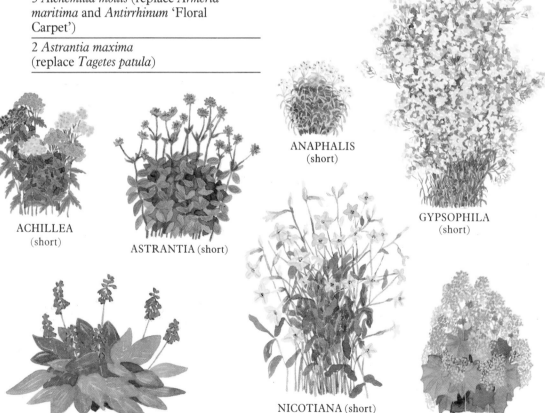

ANAPHALIS
(short)

GYPSOPHILA
(short)

ACHILLEA
(short)

ASTRANTIA (short)

NICOTIANA (short)

HOSTA (short)

ALCHEMILLA (short)

April   Prepare the bed and plant the anaphalis, achillea, hosta, gypsophila, alchemilla and astrantia as described on page 10.

May   Plant the nicotiana following the method described on page 12 after the date of the last expected frost in your area.

> **In subsequent years**, replant nicotiana annually.

Push a few twiggy brushwood sticks in round the gypsophila to support the plant if you live in a windy area.

Push a few twiggy brushwood sticks in around the nicotiana for support if you live in a windy area.

> **In subsequent years**, dig up and divide hostas, following the instructions for bergenia etc on page 19.

June, July   Cut astrantia flowers for drying soon after they open. Hang the flowers upside down in small bunches in a cool airy place out of direct sunlight.

Cut flowers that will be used fresh shortly after the buds open. Only cut a few at a time from each plant to avoid spoiling the appearance of the garden in the first year. When the plants are established, you can cut more.

August   Cut anaphalis flowers for drying soon after they open, and dry as described above.

September   Towards the end of the month, cut down the flower stems and foliage of anaphalis, achillea, gypsophila, astrantia and hosta, and remove only the stems and old leaves of alchemilla.

Pull out nicotiana when the last flowers are over.

Remove brushwood sticks if these were used as plant supports and leave the bed tidy for winter.

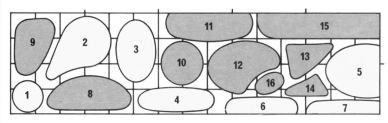

1 *Anaphalis*: August   **2** *Nicotiana*: June–September
3 *Achillea*: July–September   **4** *Hosta fortunei*: July
5 *Gypsophila*: June–August   **6** *Alchemilla*: June–August   **7** *Astrantia*
8 *Dianthus*   **9** *Sweet peas*   **10** *Astilbe*   **11** *Delphiniums*
12 *Floribunda*   **13** *Lilies*   **14** *Hostas*   **15** *Climbing rose*   **16** *Columbine*

Nutrient-Poor

The final variation shows how to turn problem soil into an asset by creating an inspiring and colourful border with plants that will thrive on dry, lifeless soil. Choose a sunny but slightly sheltered site. You will not need any stakes, plant ties or brushwood sticks for this variation.

April

4 *Hedera* 'Paddy's Pride' (replace *Lathyrus odoratus*)

4 *Lavandula spica* 'Hidcote' (lavender) (replace *Nicotiana alata* 'Sensation Mixed')

1 *Rosmarinus officinalis* 'Jessop's Upright' (rosemary) (replaces *Digitalis purpurea* 'Excelsior')

1 *Romneya coulteri* (replaces *Astilbe* 'Fanal')

3 *Stachys lanata* (replace *Petunia* 'Resisto Mixed')

4 *Bergenia* 'Ballawley' (replace *Delphinium* 'Pacific Hybrids')

1 *Sambucus racemosa* 'Plumosa Aurea' (replaces 'Elizabeth of Glamis')

3 *Liatris callilepis* (replace *Lilium regale*)

1 *Salvia purpurea* (replaces *Hosta sieboldiana* 'Elegans')

4 *Hedera* 'Paddy's Pride' (replace 'Elegance')

3 *Armeria maritima* (replace *Antirrhinum* 'Floral Carpet')

June

5 *Mesembryanthemum criniflorum* (replace *Tagetes patula*)

5 *Portulaca grandiflora* (replace *Lobelia erinus* 'Mrs Clibran')

From the garden shed

1 × 2 gal (10 litre) bucketful peat or well-rotted garden compost for mulching

HEDERA
(tall)

MESEMBRYANTHEMUM
(dwarf)

LAVANDULA (short)

ROSMARINUS
(medium)

PORTULACA (dwarf)

SALVIA (medium)

April Prepare the border and plant the hedera, lavender, rosemary, romneya, stachys, bergenia, sambucus, salvia and armeria following the instructions for astilbe etc on page 10.

Plant the liatris tubers at 2 times their own depth. After planting and watering in, mulch over the tubers with a bucket of peat or compost to retain moisture round the roots as they grow, then mark the spot with a few short sticks so you do not accidentally hoe them out.

In subsequent years, dig up and divide liatris and bergenia when the clumps become too big. Use two garden forks back to back to prise the clump apart and replant only the best, healthiest-looking pieces with lots of young growth from round the outside of the original clump.

Prune rosemary only to remove any shoots that have been damaged by cold during the winter (these will have turned brown) and to trim any branches that are growing out of shape. In both cases cut the shoots right back to their base. No other pruning is necessary.

Remove any shoots of hedera that have broken, come down off their support or turned brown. Cut them off just above a healthy leaf.

Sambucus and salvia need no regular pruning; just cut any damaged or dead shoots back to the junction with a healthy shoot.

ROMNEYA (medium)

BERGENIA (short)

STACHYS (dwarf)

LIATRIS (short)

SAMBUCUS (tall)

1 *Hedera*
2 *Lavender*: July–September
3 *Rosemary*: March–April
4 *Romneya*: July–September
5 *Stachys*: July
6 *Bergenia*: April–May
7 *Sambucus*
8 *Liatris*: July–September
9 *Salvia*   10 *Armeria*: May–July
11 *Mesembryanthemum*: June–September
12 *Portulaca*: June–September
13 *Senecio*   14 *Sedum*
15 *Dianthus*   16 *Columbine*

June   Plant out the mesembryanthemum and portulaca following the instructions for sweet peas on page 12.

> **In subsequent years**, replace portulaca and mesembryanthemum each year.

May   Train hedera up on to the wall, fence or trellis provided for it. Once it has started to climb the plant is entirely self supporting by means of the aerial roots produced from its climbing stems.

Deadhead bergenia regularly to encourage further flowers.

Spray hedera growing on a wall with plain water from a hose to help the aerial roots to grip into the brickwork. An occasional spraying will be beneficial to hedera growing on fencing, trellis or netting as well, as it will freshen it up.

Deadhead mesembryanthemum and portulaca to encourage further flowers to develop.

July   Deadhead stachys, liatris, mesembryanthemum and portulaca.

August   Deadhead armeria after all the flowers are over by clipping them off with shears, and continue deadheading the liatris, mesembryanthemum and portulaca.

September   Cut down the flower stems of liatris and stachys close to the ground when the flowers are over.

Clip lavender with shears to remove the dead flower heads and lightly reshape the plants. Do not cut back into the old wood (easily recognizable by its dark colour) or the plants may be killed.

Pull out mesembryanthemum and portulaca when the last of the flowers are over.

October   Towards the end of the month, cut down the stems of romneya almost to ground level and cover the roots with two bucketfuls of peat or bracken to protect them from frost during the winter.

Herbaceous Beds

For a garden that is a mass of flowers year after year without needing yearly replanting you can't beat herbaceous perennials. This plan shows how to create an eyecatching herbaceous bed that will always be packed with blooms throughout spring, summer and autumn. Strictly speaking, herbaceous plants are those that die down in the winter and grow up again each spring. However, the term has become extended slightly to include many sorts of low shrubby plants like helianthemum that in normal cultivation are cut back fairly hard every autumn.

Ingredients for an island bed 12ft × 13ft (3.5m × 4m)

April

2 *Acanthus mollis*

3 *Delphinium* 'Pacific Hybrids'

3 *Rudbeckia fulgida* 'Deamii'

2 *Phlox paniculata* 'Marlborough'

3 *Coreopsis verticillata*

3 *Hosta fortunei* 'Albopicta'

3 *Lupinus* 'Russell Hybrids'

1 *Gypsophila paniculata* 'Bristol Fairy'

3 *Geum chiloense* 'Mrs Bradshaw'

3 *Helianthemum nummularium*

3 *Sedum* × 'Autumn Joy'

3 *Alchemilla mollis*

2 *Solidago* 'Golden Sun'

3 *Campanula carpatica* 'Jingle Bells'

2 *Nepeta* × *faassenii*

5 *Polygonum affine* 'Donald Lowndes'

From the garden shed

Large packet of slug pellets

12 × 2 gal (10 litre) bucketfuls of peat, well-rotted manure or garden compost or bark chippings for mulching

3 × 7ft (2m) plant stakes

Bundle of 2ft (75cm) tall, twiggy pea sticks

Tools required

Spade

Fork

Rake

Garden line

Hand trowel

Hose or lawn sprinkler

Hoe

String or plant ties

Secateurs

Shears

ALCHEMILLA (short)

HOSTA (short)

DELPHINIUM (medium)

SEDUM (short)

COREOPSIS (short)

CAMPANULA (dwarf)

RUDBECKIA (short)

PHLOX
(short)

LUPINUS (short)

NEPETA (short)

ACANTHUS
(short)

POLYGONUM (dwarf)

GEUM (short)

GYPSOPHILA
(short)

HELIANTHEMUM (dwarf)

SOLIDAGO
(medium)

Above Herbaceous bed.
Left Plan for the bed. Coloured areas indicate plants in flower in midsummer. Average flowering periods are listed below:

1 *Acanthus:* July–August
2 *Delphiniums:* June–July
3 *Rudbeckia:* July–September
4 *Phlox:* July–September
5 *Coreopsis:* June–September
6 *Hostas:* July
7 *Lupins:* May–July
8 *Gypsophila:* June–August
9 *Geum:* June–August
10 *Helianthemum:* June–July
11 *Sedum:* September–October
12 *Alchemilla:* June–August
13 *Solidago:* August–September
14 *Campanula:* July–August
15 *Nepeta:* May–September
16 *Polygonum:* June

Method

Choose a site where the sun will be directly on the bed for at least half the day, as herbaceous plants are sun lovers. Start by marking the bed out using a hose (the normal technique using a garden line or four canes and some string is more difficult to apply to a bed with rounded edges). Unroll the hose and lay it roughly in position. Any irregularities in the shape are easily corrected at this stage.

Cut the bed out, using the edge of the hose as a guide. Use the spade the wrong way round so that its blade enters the soil at right angles, giving a clean, straight edge that can easily be kept tidy with shears later.

April

Before planting Stand the plants, still in pots, in their planting positions. Turn each one so that its best side faces outwards.

Planting Plant from the middle of the bed. Lift each plant in turn, mark its position with a trowel, and knock it out of its pot. A tap on the base with the handle of the trowel will quickly dislodge it. Dig a hole the same size as the pot and fit the plant's rootball into it.

Check that the best side is still facing outwards and that the top of the rootball is level with the surface of the surrounding soil before filling in round the roots with soil. Firm each plant gently in place with the handle of the trowel. Scuff out the footmarks you make with the point of the trowel.

When all the plants are in, give the whole bed a thorough watering using the hose – a lawn sprinkler makes this job very much quicker. Then spread a 'mulch' of peat, well-rotted manure or garden compost or bark chippings all over the surface of the bed. This is not strictly essential, but it is beneficial to the plants.

Finally, apply slug pellets evenly over the entire bed at the rate recommended by the manufacturers.

May

MAINTENANCE

In the first few weeks after planting check weekly to see if watering is required and, if so, use the hose or lawn sprinkler again to give the bed a thorough soaking.

Hand weed the entire herbaceous bed every 2 weeks to ensure that the plants are not smothered by weeds, which will inhibit their growth and can restrict flowering. If using a hoe take great care to avoid slicing into the stems of the plants and hoe only very shallowly to avoid cutting into the roots, which grow quite near the surface. Alternatively, use a weedkiller especially intended for use among flowers, but take care not to exceed the stated dose or it can retard the growth of your plants.

> **In subsequent years**, feed the bed with 2oz (50g) Growmore per sq yd (sq m) as soon as the plants start to show signs of growth. Snap the old flower stems of sedum off at the base.

Push a 7ft (2m) stake in alongside each delphinium, placing it on the side of the plant closest to the middle of the bed where it will be least obtrusive. Hammer the

(May)	stake 18–24 inches (46–61cm) into the ground and secure the stem to it with plant ties.
	In windy areas, support geum, rudbeckia, gypsophila, lupins and phlox by pushing two twiggy pea sticks 12 inches (30cm) into the ground beside each plant.
	Weed every 2 weeks, as in April.
	Apply slug pellets 3–4 weeks after the first application (or sooner if the weather is rainy or you are doing a lot of watering, as they dissolve).
June	Continue tying in the growing flower stems of delphiniums to ensure the flower is properly supported when it opens.
	Apply slug pellets every 3–4 weeks, more often in rainy weather. Continue weeding.
July	Tie in the flower stems of delphinium for the first few weeks. In late July, when the flowers are over, take the dead heads off partway down the stem, cutting just above a healthy-looking leaf. Do the same with lupins. Cut the dead flower heads regularly from all the plants as soon as they are over to encourage them to keep producing new blooms. Continue to apply slug pellets.
August	Cut helianthemum to within 6in (15cm) of ground level. Remove dead flower stems and foliage from polygonum.
	Apply slug pellets if necessary, and continue weeding.
September	Late in the month cut the flower stems and leaves of hosta, delphinium, lupin, gypsophila, nepeta, geum and acanthus right down to ground level and remove and burn them. Cut back coreopsis after flowering. Remove the stems and old foliage of alchemilla. Deadhead rudbeckia as flowers fade.
October	Do not remove the stems of sedum, as they are needed to give some protection to the developing young shoots early next spring.
	Remove debris from the bed and leave it tidy for winter.
November	Cut rudbeckia and solidago stems to the ground.

Blue and White

*Here the basic plan has been adapted to create a fashionable new look
– a 'monochromatic' colour scheme of blue and white flowers only.
Buy the following plants to replace those shown in brackets.*

April

2 *Chrysanthemum maximum* (Shasta daisy) (replace *Rudbeckia fulgida* 'Deamii')

2 *Phlox paniculata* 'White Admiral' (replace *Phlox paniculata* 'Marlborough')

4 *Campanula medium* 'Calycanthema' (replace *Coreopsis verticillata*)

4 *Lilium candidum* (lilies) (replace *Lupinus* 'Russell Hybrids')

2 *Salvia* × *superba* (replace *Geum chiloense* 'Mrs Bradshaw')

6 *Ajuga reptans* (replace *Helianthemum nummularium*)

4 *Nepeta* × *faassenii* (replace *Sedum* × 'Autumn Joy')

3 *Liriope muscari* (replace *Sedum* × 'Autumn Joy')

5 *Anaphalis triplinervis* (replace *Alchemilla mollis*, *Campanula carpatica* 'Jingle Bells' and 2 *Polygonum affine* 'Donald Lowndes')

2 *Geranium* 'Johnson's Blue' (replace *Solidago* 'Golden Sun')

6 *Dianthus* 'Mrs Sinkins' (replace 3 *Polygonum affine* 'Donald Lowndes')

From the garden shed

An extra bucketful of peat

CHRYSANTHEMUM
(short)

GERANIUM
(short)

DIANTHUS (short)

LILIUM
(medium)

PHLOX (short)

SALVIA (short)

AJUGA (dwarf)

CAMPANULA
(short)

LIRIOPE
(dwarf)

ANAPHALIS
(short)

1 *Chrysanthemums:* June–August   **2** *Phlox:* July–September   **3** *Campanula:* May–July   **4** *Lilies:* June–July   **5** *Salvia:* July–September   **6** *Ajuga:* June–July   **7** *Nepeta:* May–September   **8** *Anaphalis:* August   **9** *Geraniums:* July–September   **10** *Dianthus:* June   **11** *Liriope:* August–November   **12** *Gypsophila*   **13** *Acanthus*   **14** *Hostas*   **15** *Delphiniums*

April   Prepare the bed as described on page 29. Plant all plants except lilies, as described on page 29.

June   Cut off the dead flower stems of dianthus completely as soon as they are over.

July   Start regularly deadheading salvia every 2 weeks. Cut the flower stem back as far as a healthy leaf. Remove dead heads from ajuga after flowering by clipping lightly over plants with shears.

August   Cut some of the stems of anaphalis to dry as 'everlasting' flowers. Deadhead salvia every 2 weeks.

September   Towards the end of the month, cut the stems of anaphalis, chrysanthemum and phlox back almost to ground level. Pull out campanula when flowers are finished. Cut down dead flower stems and foliage on nepeta. Cut off the dead flower heads of geranium.

October   Plant the lilies. Dig a hole slightly larger than the bulb, place a handful of peat at the bottom and press the bulb firmly into this with a slight screwing motion. Fill the holes with soil, leaving the tip of each bulb showing just above the surface.

November   Cut down the flower spikes of liriope.

Pink and Silver

This variation gives another monochromatic theme, this time in pink and silver. Buy the following plants to replace those shown in brackets.

3 *Monarda didyma* 'Croftway Pink' (replace *Delphinium* Pacific Hybrids)

2 *Chrysanthemum maximum* (replace *Rudbeckia fulgida* 'Deamii')

2 *Phlox paniculata* 'Chinz' (replace *Phlox paniculata* 'Marlborough')

2 *Astrantia maxima* (replace *Coreopsis verticillata*)

3 *Pyrethrum roseum* 'Eileen May Robinson' (replace *Lupinus* 'Russell Hybrids')

3 *Heuchera sanguinea* (replace *Geum chiloense* 'Mrs Bradshaw')

3 *Stachys lanata* (replace *Helianthemum nummularium*)

3 *Armeria maritima* (replace *Sedum* × 'Autumn Joy')

2 *Bergenia* 'Ballawley Hybrids' (replace *Alchemilla mollis*)

2 *Geranium endressii* 'Wargrave Pink' (replace *Solidago* 'Golden Sun')

3 *Anaphalis triplinervis* (replace *Campanula carpatica* 'Jingle Bells')

3 *Stachys lanata* (replace *Nepeta* × *faassenii*)

6 *Dianthus* 'Doris' and 2 *Anaphalis triplinervis* (replace *Polygonum affine* 'Donald Lowndes')

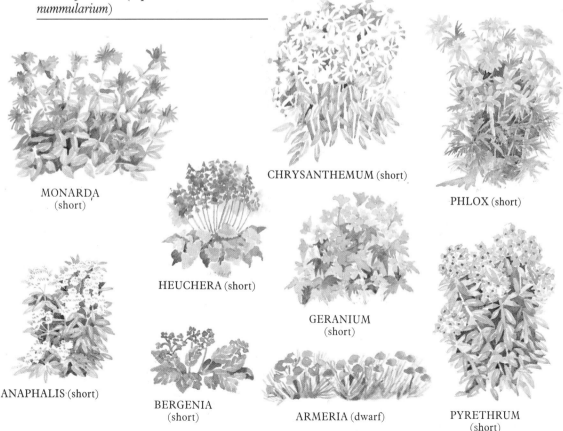

MONARDA (short)

CHRYSANTHEMUM (short)

PHLOX (short)

HEUCHERA (short)

ANAPHALIS (short)

BERGENIA (short)

GERANIUM (short)

ARMERIA (dwarf)

PYRETHRUM (short)

April   Prepare the bed as described on page 29. Plant as described on page 29, using the plants listed here.

ASTRANTIA (short)

DIANTHUS (short)

STACHYS (dwarf)

1 *Monarda*: June–September
2 *Chrysanthemums*: June–August
3 *Phlox*: July–September   **4** *Astrantia*: June–July   **5** *Pyrethrum*: June–July
6 *Heuchera*: June–September   **7** *Stachys*: July   **8** *Armeria*: May–July
9 *Bergenia*: April–May   **10** *Geraniums*: May–August   **11** *Anaphalis*: August
12 *Dianthus*: June–July, September–October   **13** *Gypsophila*   **14** *Acanthus*
15 *Hostas*

May   In windy areas, push some 2½ft (76cm) tall twiggy pea sticks into the soil around astrantia and pyrethrum.

June   Snip off the dead flower heads from dianthus and bergenia as soon as they are over.

July   Continue deadheading dianthus, and bergenia.
Late in the month cut back the flower stems of pyrethrum to encourage a second flush of flowers later.

August   Snip the dead flower stems from armeria.

September   Towards the end of the month, cut the stems of astrantia, monarda, geranium, phlox and chrysanthemum down almost to ground level.
Remove the flower stems only of heuchera and stachys, leaving the foliage.
Select straggly or broken dianthus shoots and cut back to their base using secateurs.

> **In subsequent years**, you may find heuchera plants have grown so that their crowns are raised slightly above the level of the surrounding soil. If this happens, tuck a handful or two of peat or garden compost under and round them for them to root back into.

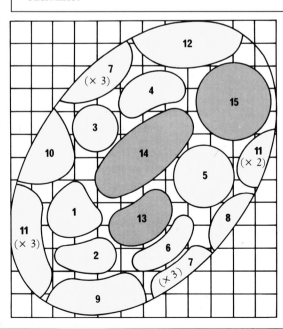

For an 18ft × 13ft (5.3m × 4m) Bed

This is a longer version of the basic plan, suitable for a larger garden. The shape of the bed and the planting plan are much the same, except that extra plants have been added to elongate the bed. You will not need geum, but you will need the following extra plants.

April

2 extra *Lupinus* 'Russell Hybrids' (lupin) (5 altogether)

2 *Bergenia* 'Ballawley Hybrids'

1 extra *Sedum* × 'Autumn Joy'

3 *Chrysanthemum maximum*

2 *Salvia* × *superba*

4 *Aster novi-belgii* 'Little Pink Beauty' (Michaelmas daisy)

3 *Geranium* 'Johnson's Blue'

2 *Stachys lanata*

STACHYS

CHRYSANTHEMUM (short)

SALVIA
(short)

GERANIUM
(short)

BERGENIA (short)

ASTER (short)

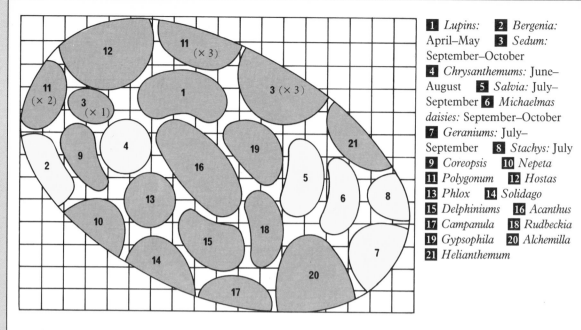

1 *Lupins:* 2 *Bergenia:* April–May 3 *Sedum:* September–October 4 *Chrysanthemums:* June–August 5 *Salvia:* July–September 6 *Michaelmas daisies:* September–October 7 *Geraniums:* July–September 8 *Stachys:* July 9 *Coreopsis* 10 *Nepeta* 11 *Polygonum* 12 *Hostas* 13 *Phlox* 14 *Solidago* 15 *Delphiniums* 16 *Acanthus* 17 *Campanula* 18 *Rudbeckia* 19 *Gypsophila* 20 *Alchemilla* 21 *Helianthemum*

April Prepare and plant the bed as described on page 29, adding the extra plants listed here.

> Replacement and additional plants are given at the start of each variation. For quantities of 'original' plants, uncoloured in the planting plan and not given in the variation ingredients, check with the list at the start of the main plan.

May Push 2½ft (76cm) tall twiggy pea sticks into the soil around the asters to give the plants some support.

June, July, August Snip off the dead flower heads of bergenia, and from then on remove the deadheads from any flowers in the bed as they die as a matter of routine.

September Towards the end of the month, cut the stems of geranium and chrysanthemum, and the leaves of bergenia, down to ground level.

Deadhead salvia after flowering is finished.

Remove the flower stems only of stachys, leaving the foliage.

October When all the flowers of aster are finished, cut the stems down to ground level.

> **In subsequent years**, in **March**, dig up clumps of aster and divide them, using two garden forks placed back to back to lever them apart. Select healthy pieces from the outside of the clump to replant, and repeat this process annually as the plants deteriorate otherwise.
>
> Every 3–4 years, dig up and divide stachys, chrysanthemum and bergenia.

Beside a Wall, Hedge or Fence

For gardens without room for an island bed, or where a more traditional herbaceous border is called for, try this final variation – an oblong bed to border a wall, fence or hedge. You do not need to buy hosta, geum or solidago.

April
1 *Acanthus mollis* (replaces 2)
2 *Polygonum affine* 'Donald Lowndes' (replace 5)
2 *Sedum* × 'Autumn Joy' (replace 3)
2 *Coreopsis verticillata* (replace 3)

From the garden shed
An extra bundle of 2½ft (76cm) tall, twiggy pea sticks
Garden line

April   Prepare and plant the bed as on page 29, following the plan below.

Immediately after planting the border, be sure to apply slug pellets. Be especially thorough about this if the border backs on to a hedge, and throw extra slug pellets as far under the hedge as you can reach. In addition, puff pest and disease dust under the hedge. At the same time, trim the hedge.

May   Push pea sticks in around all of the plants in the back row of the border (except the delphiniums, which should have stakes put in beside them). In windy areas push sticks in round the plants in the middle row as well.

June, July, August   Water regularly.

October   After the herbaceous bed has been cleared of most of its foliage, clean out any weeds and rubbish from the bottom of the hedge behind it and trim it – or do any repairs necessary to the fence or wall, whichever is appropriate. Apply preservative to a fence, using a brand known to be non-toxic to plants rather than creosote.

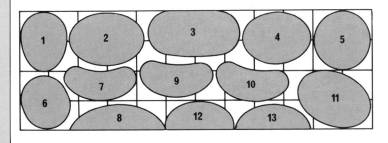

1 *Phlox*   2 *Lupins*   3 *Acanthus*
4 *Delphiniums*   5 *Rudbeckia*
6 *Nepeta*   7 *Sedum*
8 *Helianthemum*
9 *Gypsophila*   10 *Coreopsis*
11 *Alchemilla*   12 *Polygonum*
13 *Campanula*

Herb Gardens

Herbs not only play a valuable role in the kitchen, they add a heady fragrance to the garden. Small but formal, this design contains a selection of herbs chosen for foliage and flower display as well as for culinary use. They are arranged round a centrepiece, which adds a focal point to the design.

Ingredients for a herb garden 6ft × 6ft (2m × 2m)

May

2 Fennel (*Foeniculum vulgare*)

3 Basil (*Ocimum basilicum*)

2 Sage (*Salvia officinalis*)

3 Chives (*Allium schoenoprasum*)

3 Dill (*Peucedanum graveolens*)

3 Sweet marjoram (*Origanum majorana*)

3 Thyme (*Thymus vulgaris*)

5 Golden marjoram (*Origanum vulgare* 'Aureum')

2 Parsley (*Petroselinum crispum*)

1 Apple mint (*Mentha rotundifolia*)

1 Spearmint (*Mentha spicata*)

From the garden shed

4 × 2 gal (10 litre) bucketfuls of coarse gravel

70 engineering bricks

1 sundial

Concrete paving slab and cement (optional)

4 small ornamental terracotta pots (frost resistant)

4 broken crocks

Small packet of slug pellets

Peat, leaf mould or straw, for winter protection

Tools required

Spade

Fork

Rake

Garden line, or 25ft (7.5m) of twine and four short pieces of cane

Hand trowel

Watering can or hose

Hoe

Secateurs

Cane or sharp sand

SAGE (short)

GOLDEN MARJORAM
(short)

THYME (dwarf)

DILL (medium)

SWEET MARJORAM
(short)

BASIL (short)

SPEARMINT
(short)

PARSLEY
(short)

FENNEL
(tall)

CHIVES
(dwarf)

APPLE MINT
(short)

Method

Choose a sunny but sheltered site and mark out a square 6ft × 6ft (2m × 2m) using a garden line and canes. Cut alongside the line with the spade. Use the spade the wrong way round so the blade goes into the soil vertically as this gives you a nice clean edge against which to set the border of bricks. Remove the line, and prepare the soil as described in the introduction.

Mark out the shape of the design using the point of a cane or by dribbling sharp sand on to the ground. Lay the engineering bricks round the edge of the garden, and make two brick paths that cross in the centre. Set the bricks into the soil firmly, 'planting' them with a trowel so that two-thirds of each brick is below the soil surface. Then place the sundial carefully in position in the centre of the bed where the two paths cross. If it is a little unsteady you can stand it on a concrete paving slab instead of bricks, anchoring it in place with a dab of cement. Spread a bucketful of coarse gravel in each of the four quarter-circles at the centre of the design, where the paths meet.

May

Planting Plant the parsley and the mint in the terracotta pots. Stand the plants, in their original container, in the ornamental pots to check for size. Put a piece of broken crock over the drainage hole of each pot, followed by sufficient compost to raise the rootball to about 1 inch (2.5cm) below the level of the rim. Knock the plants out of their containers by tapping them on the base with a trowel and repot them, filling in with soil as necessary. Stand them on the gravel near the sundial in the centre.

Now check with the plan and stand the fennel, basil, sage, chives, dill, thyme, sweet marjoram and golden marjoram in position, still in their pots, where they are to be planted. Make sure that they are the right distances apart, and turn each one so that its best side faces outwards in the direction it will normally be seen from.

MAINTENANCE

Herbs are very slow growing, particularly during their first year, and need a certain amount of attention to help them become successfully established. For the first few weeks after planting, always water them during dry weather.

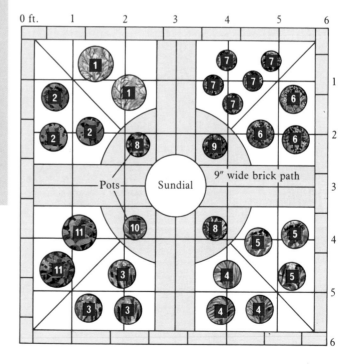

Above opposite Herb garden.   **Right** Plan for the herb garden.   **1** *Fennel*   **2** *Basil*   **3** *Chives*   **4** *Dill*   **5** *Sweet marjoram*   **6** *Thyme*   **7** *Golden marjoram*   **8** *Parsley*   **9** *Apple mint*   **10** *Spearmint*   **11** *Sage*

Plant from the centre of the bed. Lift each pot in turn and mark its position with the trowel. Gently knock it out of its pot by tapping its base with the trowel and dig a hole the same depth as the pot, as marked. Taking care not to break up the ball of roots, place the plant into its hole. Check that its best side is still facing the right way, then use the trowel to fill in round the roots with soil. Firm round the plant with the trowel handle after planting.

When you have planted the whole bed, water in each plant with approximately 1pt (500ml) of water. Spread a layer of peat or compost 1 inch (2.5cm) deep between the plants. Sprinkle a few slug pellets between plants.

In subsequent years, replant dill, basil and parsley at this time.

Special note

When you have finished planting it is advisable to spread a thin layer of peat or well-rotted garden compost between the plants. Mulching, as this is called, has many beneficial effects; it smothers weed seedlings, improves the soil by adding organic matter to it, insulates the roots of the plants from heat in summer and cold in winter and helps to retain moisture in the soil (particularly important in the case of annuals, which are very shallow-rooted). It also provides a pleasingly uniform dark background to the plants. Mulch again every spring as the growing season begins.

June	Hoe or hand weed the garden once a week to prevent any weeds from taking hold and always sprinkle a few slug pellets around the plants after hoeing or watering; the original pellets will soon become dissolved by rain or buried when you disturb the soil.
July	Pinch out flowers with your thumb and index finger, as soon as they begin to form (you may want to allow dill and fennel to flower so that you can collect the seeds for culinary use). Continue weeding and watering and apply slug pellets in rainy weather. Check for aphids.
September	Pull out the basil and dill as they begin to die. Cut the chives down to ground level and pull out the parsley as the leaves turn yellow. Prune any untidy branches on the thyme and sage back to the main stem. Cut down fennel stems after collecting seed for culinary use.
October	If you live in a cold district, cover the marjoram with a protective layer of peat, leaf mould or straw. The mints will die back in winter and reappear in spring.

> **In subsequent years**, in **March**, scatter 1oz (25g) of Growmore fertilizer to each sq yd (sq m) of bed (optional), and start hoeing out weeds, as soon as new growth appears.

Classical

In this variation a more classical look, reminiscent of the English knot gardens of old, is achieved by replacing the border of bricks in the original plan with a low-trimmed box hedge.

May

1 Sage (*Salvia officinalis*)

2 Chives (*Allium schoenoprasum*)

2 Sweet marjoram (*Origanum majorana*)

2 Dill (*Peucedanum graveolens*)

3 Thyme (*Thymus vulgaris*)

1 Apple mint (*Mentha rotundifolia*)

4 Parsley (*Petroselinum crispum*)

2 Basil (*Ocimum basilicum*)

100 trained *Buxus sempervirens suffruticosa* (box) plants 4 inches (10cm) wide for edging (if unobtainable already trained, buy small bushy young plants and train your own).

From the garden shed

Hedging shears

Large plastic bag or old bucket

34 engineering bricks for path

May   Plant the sage, chives, sweet marjoram, dill, thyme, parsley and basil following the instructions for sage etc on page 40.

   Plant the apple mint. Dig a hole deep enough and wide enough to take the mint's roots, and line with a plastic bag. Fill the bag with soil, and plant the mint in it, following instructions for sage etc on page 40. This prevents the roots from spreading. Alternatively, dig a hole big enough to take an old bucket, fill the bucket with soil and plant the apple mint in this container.

   Plant box hedging in place of the brick boundary and around the outline of the beds, following the instructions for sage etc on page 40. Space the plants 6 inches (15cm) apart.

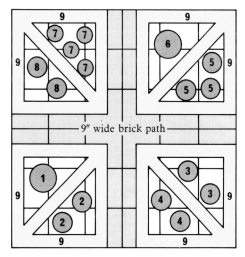

9" wide brick path

1 Sage   **2** Chives   **3** Sweet marjoram
4 Dill   **5** Thyme   **6** Apple mint
7 Parsley   **8** Basil   **9** Box hedging

July, August   Clip the box with shears every 6–8 weeks to gradually form the shape of the hedge. Subsequently clip as often as necessary to keep it tidy, and about 4 inches (10cm) wide and 1ft (30cm) high.

BUXUS

Decorative

In this variation herbs have been chosen primarily for their ornamental rather than culinary value; many of them can, nevertheless, be used in certain recipes. The general effect creates a picturesque cottage-style herb garden full of old world charm. The space occupied by the bordering lavender hedge means that fewer plants are required to fill the central beds. You will not need the coarse gravel, boundary bricks or small terracotta pots.

March

1 Standard trained bay tree (*Laurus nobilis*)

1 Angelica (*Angelica archangelica*)

1 Rue (*Ruta graveolens* 'Jackman's Blue')

15 Dwarf lavender (*Lavandula spica* 'Hidcote')

May

3 Parsley (*Petroselinum crispum*)

2 Chives (*Allium schoenoprasum*)

1 Sweet cicely (*Myrrhis odorata*)

1 Sage (*Salvia officinalis*)

1 Fennel (*Foeniculum vulgare*)

2 Sweet marjoram (*Origanum majorana*)

From the garden shed

Hedging shears

38 engineering bricks

Large ornamental terracotta pot or wooden tub

Bag of John Innes potting compost

LAVANDULA (short)

BAY TREE
(tall)

RUE (short)

SWEET CICELY
(short)

ANGELICA (tall)

Follow the method described in the original plan for laying the brick paths, but add an extra two bricks to two of the central corners where the paths cross.

March   Plant the lavender hedge following the instructions for sage etc on page 40, spacing the plants 10 inches (25cm) apart.

Plant out the angelica and rue following the instructions for sage etc on page 40. Cover the drainage hole of the ornamental pot with crocks and add some compost. Knock the container of the bay tree against a hard surface and lift the tree out carefully. Repot in the ornamental container, filling with soil as necessary. Position the tree in the centre of the garden.

> **In subsequent years**, replant the angelica every second year.

May   Plant out the parsley, chives, sweet cicely, sage, fennel and sweet marjoram following the instructions for sage etc on page 40.

> **In subsequent years**, replant the parsley at this time.

Replacement and additional plants are given at the start of each variation. For quantities of 'original' plants, uncoloured in the planting plan and not given in the variation ingredients, check with the list at the start of the main plan.

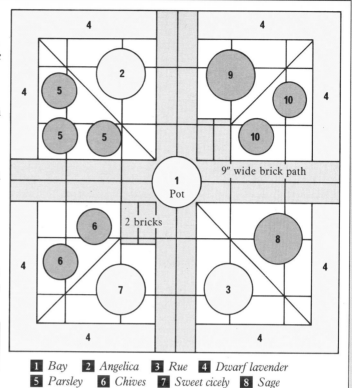

9″ wide brick path

2 bricks

1	Bay	2	Angelica	3	Rue	4	Dwarf lavender
5	Parsley	6	Chives	7	Sweet cicely	8	Sage
9	Fennel	10	Sweet marjoram				

September   Trim the lavender hedge into shape using hedging shears; this will also be sufficient to remove the dead flower heads. Move the bay tree to a very sheltered place for the winter – a cold greenhouse or porch is ideal. Remove dead flower heads from rue.

> **In subsequent years**, in **April**, trim the rue back to old (darker) wood to keep the plant's bushy shape.
>
> In **September**, as the lavender plants become more mature, take care not to cut back into the old, dark-coloured wood near the base of the plants. Instead, just clip the soft shoots of the current season's growth. Check the bay tree each year to see if it needs transplanting to a larger pot.

Herb Border

A selection of ornamental and culinary herbs from the previous designs, together with a few new varieties, create an attractive and productive garden bed measuring 15ft × 4ft (5m × 1.2m). It is suitable for a sunny situation bordering a wall, fence or hedge. You will not need bricks, ornamental pots or gravel, but you will need more compost, manure or peat, sharp sand and fertilizer.

March

2 Dwarf lavender (*Lavandula spica* 'Hidcote')

1 Ox-eye chamomile (*Anthemis tinctoria* 'Grallagh Gold')

1 Angelica (*Angelica archangelica*)

1 Rue (*Ruta graveolens* 'Jackman's Blue')

1 Rosemary (*Rosmarinus officinalis* 'Jessop's Upright')

1 French sorrel (*Rumex scutatus*)

April

1 Standard trained bay tree (*Laurus nobilis*)

May

1 Apple mint (*Mentha rotundifolia*)

1 Thyme (*Thymus vulgaris*)

4 Chives (*Allium schoenoprasum*)

3 Basil (*Ocimum purpurea* 'Dark Opal')

3 Basil (*Ocimum basilicum*)

1 Sage (*Salvia officinalis*)

3 Dill (*Peucedanum graveolens*)

5 Parsley (*Petroselinum crispum*)

3 Sweet cicely (*Myrrhis odorata*)

1 Sage (*Salvia officinalis* 'Tricolor')

5 Nasturtiums (*Tropaeolum majus*)

3 Golden marjoram (*Origanum vulgare* 'Aureum')

From the garden shed

15 × 2 gal (10 litre) bucketfuls peat, well-rotted manure or garden compost

6–7 × 2 gal (10 litre) bucketfuls sharp sand or gravel (for clay soil)

6oz (185g) Growmore fertilizer

5 pea sticks 6ft (2m) high

Large plastic bag or an old bucket

Edging shears

LAVENDER (short)

SAGE 'Tricolor' (short)

NASTURTIUM (tall)

ROSEMARY (medium)

SORREL (short)

BASIL 'Dark Opal'
(short)

CHAMOMILE
(short)

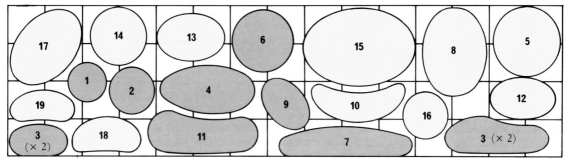

March   Plant out the herbs listed under March, as instructed for sage etc on page 40.

> **In subsequent years**, replant the angelica every year.

April   Plant the bay tree in its pot to facilitate moving it for the winter. Dig a hole and sink the pot into it.

May   Plant out all 'May' herbs except mint, following the instructions for sage etc on page 40. Provide pea sticks for the nasturtiums.

Plant the apple mint as described on page 43 to prevent the roots from becoming too invasive.

1 *Apple mint*   **2** *Thyme*   **3** *Chives*   **4** *Basil*
5 *Sage*   **6** *Dill*   **7** *Parsley*   **8** *Sweet cicely*
9 *Sage 'Tricolor'*   **10** *Nasturtiums*   **11** *Golden marjoram*
12 *Lavender*   **13** *Bay tree*   **14** *Chamomile*   **15** *Angelica*
16 *Rue*   **17** *Rosemary*   **18** *French sorrel*
19 *Basil 'Dark Opal'*

> **In subsequent years**, in **May**, prune rosemary and sages; cut out broken or untidy branches to a main branch. In **September**, cut back lavender lightly with shears.

June, July, August   Pinch out flowering stems of sorrel, as they appear.

September   Pull out the nasturtiums and basils as they begin to die.

October   Cut down old flower stems of chamomile.

Herb Containers

Herbs in containers can be fitted into the tiniest of gardens, using any hardstanding area – perhaps beside a back door or on a patio – in a reasonably sheltered sunny location. You need no soil improvers or fertilizer. Use only the following plants:

April

1 standard trained bay tree (*Laurus nobilis*)

May

1 Sage (*Salvia officinalis*)

1 Parsley (*Petroselinum crispum*)

1 Basil (*Ocimum basilicum*)

1 Spearmint (*Mentha rotundifolia*)

1 Sweet marjoram (*Origanum majorana*)

1 Chives (*Allium schoenoprasum*)

1 Thyme (*Thymus vulgaris*)

From the garden shed

1 windowbox measuring 3ft × 9 inches (1m × 23cm)

1 × 18 inch (46cm) diameter terracotta pot

2 × 9 inch (23cm) diameter terracotta pots

2 × 5 inch (13 cm) diameter terracotta pots (all frost resistant and with drainage holes)

1 large bag of John Innes potting compost

Liquid pot plant feed

Stiff brush for cleaning pots

BAY (tall)

1 Sage **2** Parsley **3** Basil **4** Spearmint
5 Sweet marjoram **6** Chives **7** Thyme **8** Bay

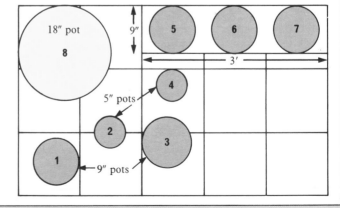

April   Repot the bay tree into the 18 inch (46cm) diameter pot. Cover the drainage hole with old crock and add compost. Knock the bay tree container against a hard surface and lift the tree out carefully. Stand in the new pot, fill in with compost and firm down.

May   Secure the windowbox in place. Stand the pots in position and half fill all the containers with potting compost. Knock the herbs out of their pots and place the mint and sage in the centre of the 9 inch (23cm) pots and the parsley and basil in the centre of the 5 inch (13cm) pots. Stand the marjoram, chives and thyme in a row along the centre of the windowbox. Then fill round the edges with more compost, finishing with the surface of the rootball level with the surface of the compost. Firm the compost down slightly with your fingers, and water each plant in: about 1pt (500ml) of water for each of the smaller pots, 2pts (1 litre) for the large ones and 3pts (1.75 litres) for the windowbox.

> **In subsequent years**, replant new parsley and basil plants.

Check every day to see if more water is needed. You can test very easily by sticking your finger into the compost or, alternatively, buy a water meter. Take care not to overwater herbs grown in containers – the compost should almost dry out between waterings. In rainy weather watering may not be needed for some time, but during hot dry spells you may need to water every day.

> **In subsequent years**, clean the outside of the pots when necessary with a stiff brush and warm water, adding a little liquid detergent if need be to remove stubborn grime. Take care not to get any inside the pots.

July   Give plants a liquid plant feed once a week.

September   As plant growth slows down, discontinue the feeds and restrict the amount of water. Basil and parsley can be thrown away after they stop producing usable leaves, and the old leaves of the chives should be cut down when they die back. The containers can remain where they are for the winter, provided they are not standing under drips or in puddles of water.

December, January, February   It is necessary to prevent the roots of plants in containers from freezing in very severe weather. The pots can be 'lagged' by wrapping them round with newspaper or old curtains, but if a sheltered porch or cold greenhouse is available, they are best stood inside for the very worst of the winter. Bay should always be stood under cover. A shed or garage is better than nothing – but do not leave plants there too long or they will soon suffer from the lack of light.

Old-Fashioned Borders

The old world charm of cottage gardens is back in vogue, and this chapter looks at the elements that make up such a garden – 'old-fashioned' scented roses, aromatic and traditional garden plants. The main plan is for a 'classic' old-fashioned border containing a little of everything.

Ingredients for a border 10ft × 4ft (3m × 1.2m)

April

1 *Rosa* 'Madame Isaac Pereire' (Bourbon)

1 *Clematis montana*

3 *Verbascum bombyciferum* 'Silver Lining'

2 *Geranium* 'Johnson's Blue'

1 *Geranium* 'Wargrave Pink'

3 *Aster novi-belgii* (Michaelmas daisy)

3 *Campanula medium* (Canterbury bells)

3 *Althaea rosea* (hollyhock)

5 *Lathyrus odoratus* 'Antique Fantasy Mixed' (sweet peas)

3 *Lupinus* 'Russell Hybrids' (lupins)

1 *Alchemilla mollis*

4 *Dianthus* 'Mrs Sinkins'

3 *Delphinium* 'Pacific Hybrids'

From the garden shed

Small packet of slug pellets

10 × 2 gal (10 litre) bucketfuls of peat, or well-rotted garden compost or manure for mulching (optional)

Drum of soil pests killer

6 × 7ft (2m) plant stakes

Plant ties

Bundle of 2½ft (76cm) tall twiggy pea sticks

Weedkiller (optional)

Rose insecticide, rose fungicide

Tools required

Spade

Fork

Rake

Garden line

Hand trowel

Watering can or hose

Secateurs

Hoe

ROSA (tall)

CLEMATIS (tall)

ALTHAEA (medium)

CAMPANULA
(short)

ALCHEMILLA (short)

ASTER (medium)

GERANIUM
'Johnson's Blue'
(short)

DIANTHUS
(short)

GERANIUM
'Wargrave Pink'
(short)

LATHYRUS (tall)

VERBASCUM
(medium)

DELPHINIUM
(medium)

LUPINUS (short)

Method

Choose a site where the sun will shine directly on to the bed for at least half the day. A border such as this would traditionally be backed by a wall or a fence, with a lawn or path bordering it. However, it could also be cut into a lawn near the rear of the garden and given an 'artificial' back by putting up a series of posts supporting wires, trellis or plastic-covered wire netting on to which the clematis and rose could be trained later.

Mark the shape of the bed out with a garden line or four canes and a ball of string. If the bed is in a lawn, cut round the edge of the bed using a spade the wrong way round to get a nice vertical edge. This will then be easy to keep tidy by trimming with edging shears later. Prepare the soil as described in the introduction.

April

Before planting Prune the rose 'Madame Isaac Pereire'. To do this, cut the thickest stems down to 12 inches (30cm) above the top of the pot, and the thinner shoots to 4 inches (10cm). Cut out any very spindly, dead or damaged shoots entirely.

Water all the plants thoroughly 12 hours or so before planting.

Stand the plants, still in pots, in their planting positions. Turn each plant so that its best side faces outwards, towards the front of the bed.

Planting Plant from the back of the bed. Lift each plant in turn and mark its position with a trowel. Then using the pot as a guide, dig a hole the same size as the pot so that the rim is level with the surface of the surrounding soil.

Now knock the plant out of its container. If it is a rigid one, a sharp tap on the base with the handle of the trowel will quickly dislodge it.

If it is the polythene bag type, cut it away without breaking up the ball of roots inside.

Sit the plant into the hole you have made, check that its best side is still facing outwards and that the top of the rootball is level with the surface of the soil. Then fill in round the roots with soil. Firm each plant gently in place with the handle of the trowel.

As you plant, scuff out footmarks.

MAINTENANCE

Mulch the bed by spreading a thin layer of peat, well-rotted manure or garden compost all over the surface. This is not essential, but it is beneficial to the plants.

Scatter slug pellets evenly over the entire bed at the rate recommended by the manufacturers.

Check weekly to see if watering is required.

Weed the bed every 2 weeks to ensure the plants are not smothered by weeds, which would inhibit their growth and flowering. If you are using a hoe take great care to avoid slicing into the stems of the plants – at this stage, they may not recover from such injury – and hoe very shallowly to avoid cutting into the roots.

Alternatively, you could use a residual weedkiller of the sort especially intended for use among flowers, but take care not to exceed the stated dose or it can retard the growth of your plants. Check with the instructions.

In subsequent years, dig up and divide geranium plants and Michaelmas daisies when they get too big, replanting them in the same place as previously. Use two garden forks, back to back, to lever the clump apart. Replant only the best pieces with lots of young growth from round the outside of the clump.

Feed the bed with 2oz (50g) Growmore per sq yd (sq m) as soon as the plants start to show signs of growth and apply slug pellets.

Control weeds. Mulch round clematis by spreading a bucketful of peat over its roots to help keep them permanently moist during the summer.

Keep the new plants well watered for the first 6–8 weeks after planting and check them subsequently during dry spells. Established plants are unlikely to need watering except in prolonged droughts.

Above Old-fashioned border. **Below** Planting plan. Coloured areas indicate plants in flower in midsummer. Average flowering periods are listed below: **1** *Bourbon rose:* June–July, September–October **2** *Clematis:* May **3** *Verbascum:* June–July **4** *Geranium* 'Johnson's Blue': July–September **5** *Geranium* 'Wargrave Pink': May–August **6** *Michaelmas daisies:* September–October **7** *Campanula:* May–July **8** *Hollyhocks:* July–September **9** *Sweet peas:* June–September **10** *Lupins:* May–July **11** *Alchemilla:* June–August **12** *Dianthus:* June **13** *Delphiniums:* June–July

(April)

Water the plants once they are all in, giving each one about 1pt (500ml) of water, apart from the rose and clematis, which should have 1 gal (4.5 litres) each. Use a watering can or hose and, if the soil is very dry, soak the entire bed.

> **In subsequent years**, plant new verbascum, sweet peas and campanula.

May

Support delphiniums and hollyhocks by pushing a 7ft (2m) stake in behind each plant, where it will be least obtrusive. Hammer the stake 18–24 inches (46–61cm) into the ground and secure the stem to it with plant ties.

Support sweet peas by pushing two 2½ft (76cm) high twiggy pea sticks in beside each plant. There is no need to tie them, as sweet peas produce tendrils that cling on to the sticks without help.

In windy areas, provide pea sticks for lupins and Michaelmas daisies too. These should be pushed 12 inches (30cm) into the ground.

Continue to apply slug pellets regularly, every 3 weeks or so, if the weather remains wet.

Weed the bed every 2 weeks.

Water every week if necessary.

> **In subsequent years**, when the flowers of clematis are over the plant can be pruned to restrict it from growing. Simply shorten the shoots that are too long by the required amount.

June

Tie the clematis to its support as it grows to help it start to climb over the fence or trellis. Encourage it to form a backdrop to the rose.

Tie the developing flower stems of delphiniums to their stakes to ensure the flowers are straight when open.

Spray the rose regularly with a systemic insecticide against greenfly and a rose fungicide against blackspot and mildew. Deadhead the rose regularly every week to encourage further flowering, cutting the stem just above the topmost leaf.

Deadhead dianthus when the flowers are over, removing the flower stem completely.

(June)	Cut off the dead flower stems from sweet peas throughout the summer to promote the development of new buds and encourage the plants to flower continuously. Continue applying slug pellets in wet weather; and weed regularly every 2 weeks.
July	Deadhead the delphiniums and lupins when the flowers are over. Cut the dead heads off partway down the stem, just above a healthy-looking leaf. In this way you can sometimes coax the plants to produce a few more flowers. Continue deadheading the rose, and sweet peas. Continue tying in clematis and hollyhocks. Spray rose against greenfly, blackspot and mildew.
August	Continue tying the hollyhock flowers to their stakes, and deadheading the sweet peas.
September In subsequent years, spray Michaelmas daisies with a fungicide if they are affected by mildew.	Deadhead the rose, which in a good summer will be producing a second flush of flowers now. Be prepared to start spraying the plant if patches of mildew (which looks like talcum powder) appear on the foliage. Cut down the flower stems and leaves of delphiniums, lupins and geraniums to ground level towards the end of the month after they have finished flowering. Cut back the flower stems and old foliage only of alchemilla, when flowering finishes. Pull out campanula, sweet peas, verbascum and hollyhocks after all their flowers are finished. Clear away weeds, stakes, pea sticks etc.
October	Prune the rose as soon as the last flowers are over: cut to ground level the thinnest of the stems that have flowered this summer and tie the new shoots that have grown up over the summer in their place. The remaining stems that flowered should have their sideshoots cut back to within 2–3 leaves of where they join the main stem. Cut the stems of Michaelmas daisies to ground level after flowering. Remove pea sticks. **In subsequent years**, prune the rose by cutting to ground level all the old, diseased and damaged stems, and any that are overcrowded. Then tie in the young shoots that have grown over the summer, in their place. No other pruning is needed.

Scented

Any old-fashioned border worthy of its name is faintly aromatic, but this variation contains plants selected especially for their scent. The design is the same as before, but some of the plants have changed to give a garden with an extra dimension. You will not need any stakes or plant ties for this border.

April

1 *Lonicera fragrantissima* (honeysuckle) (replaces *Clematis montana*)

4 *Lilium regale* (lily) (replace *Verbascum bombyciferum* 'Silver Lining')

2 *Nepeta* × *faassenii* (replace *Geranium* 'Johnson's Blue')

12 *Malcolmia maritima* or a packet of seed (Virginian stock) (replace *Geranium* 'Wargrave Pink')

1 *Origanum vulgare* 'Aureum' (golden marjoram), and
3 *Viola* 'Violet Queen' (pansy)
   (replace *Aster novi-belgii*)

6 *Reseda odorata* (mignonette) (replace *Campanula medium*)

3 *Monarda didyma* 'Croftway Pink' (replace *Lupinus* 'Russell Hybrids')

1 *Lavandula spica* 'Hidcote' (replaces *Alchemilla mollis*)

3 *Hesperis matronalis* (replace *Delphinium* 'Pacific Hybrids')

May

6 *Nicotiana alata* 'Sensation Mixed' (replace *Althaea rosea*)

From the garden shed

Extra pea sticks

Tools required

Shears

HESPERIS (short)

NICOTIANA (short)

LAVANDULA (short)

RESEDA
(short)

LONICERA
(medium)

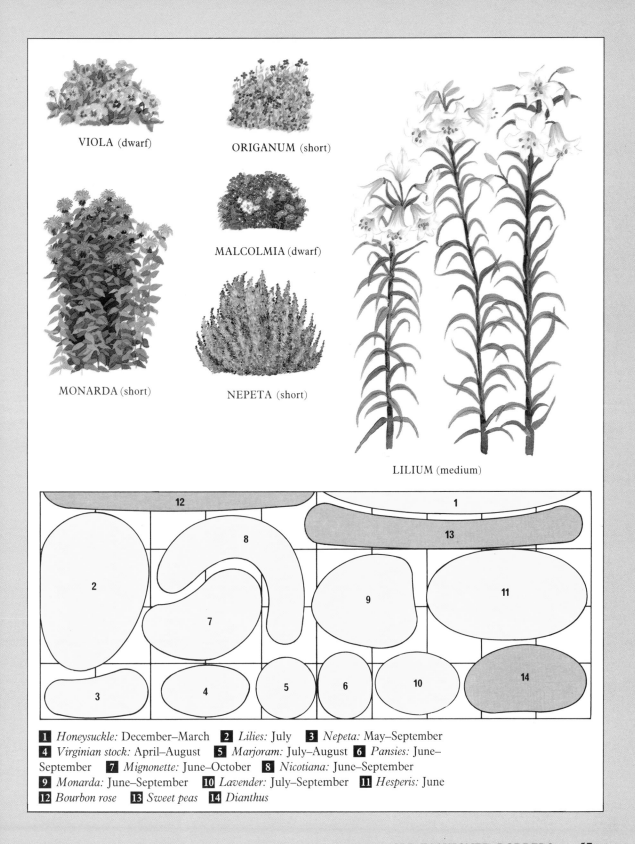

VIOLA (dwarf)

ORIGANUM (short)

MALCOLMIA (dwarf)

MONARDA (short)

NEPETA (short)

LILIUM (medium)

1 *Honeysuckle:* December–March   **2** *Lilies:* July   **3** *Nepeta:* May–September
4 *Virginian stock:* April–August   **5** *Marjoram:* July–August   **6** *Pansies:* June–
September   **7** *Mignonette:* June–October   **8** *Nicotiana:* June–September
9 *Monarda:* June–September   **10** *Lavender:* July–September   **11** *Hesperis:* June
12 *Bourbon rose*   **13** *Sweet peas*   **14** *Dianthus*

April   Prepare the bed and plant the honeysuckle, nepeta, Virginian stock, marjoram, pansies, mignonette, monarda, lavender and hesperis following the instructions on page 52.

To plant the lily bulbs, dig holes 9 inches (23 cm) deep and sprinkle a little compost at the bottom of the holes. Put a bulb in each, pointed end up, and settle it into the compost with a slight twisting motion. Fill in with soil and firm the soil down with the handle of the trowel.

Sow seeds of Virginian stock if plants are not available. Rake the area to produce a fine tilth, then scatter the seeds thinly and rake over the area lightly to cover the seeds. Water well.

> **In subsequent years**, replant mignonette, Virginian stock and pansies.

May   Plant out the nicotiana following the instructions on page 52 after the last danger of frost has passed.

> **In subsequent years**, replant nicotiana.

> Replacement and additional plants are given at the start of each variation. For quantities of 'original' plants, uncoloured in the planting plan and not given in the variation ingredients, check with the list at the start of the main plan.

There is no need to thin out the Virginian stock seedlings when they come up, and the plants may start flowering in as little as 4 weeks.

> **In subsequent years**, dig up and divide monarda at the beginning of the month. This will need doing every 2–3 years to maintain the vigour of the plants. Divide them by using two garden forks back to back to lever the clump apart. Replant only those pieces with young growth from round the edge of the clump.
> Mulch the honeysuckle following the instructions for clematis on page 52.
> Mulch between the lilies, taking care not to break off any young shoots.
> Prune the honeysuckle if it becomes overgrown or straggly. Simply cut back as required to a maximum of 50 per cent of the size of the plant, always cutting just above the leaf joints. Regular pruning is not necessary.

Support nicotiana and hesperis by pushing pea sticks in between the plants. In windy areas support the lilies, monarda and mignonette in the same way.

June, July, August   Deadhead the pansies regularly, snipping off the flower stems.

Do not, however, remove the dead flower heads from hesperis and Virginian stock, as the plants will shed seed that will eventually replace the parents.

September   Cut down and remove the dead flower stems and foliage from the lilies, nepeta and monarda.

Pull out Virginian stock, nicotiana and pansies as soon as their flowers are finished.

> **In subsequent years**, clip lavender lightly with shears after the flowers are over to remove the dead heads and reshape the plants. Do not prune back into the old, dark-coloured wood.
> Cut back marjoram by about half its height if it is untidy or full of woody stems and dead flower heads.

October   Pull out mignonette after flowering.

Traditional

This variation concentrates particularly on species plants, simple flowers and old-fashioned aromatics to give a border with an especially traditional air about it. Buy the following plants, which replace those shown in brackets from our original list.

April

3 *Lathyrus latifolius* (everlasting sweet pea) (replace *Clematis montana* and *Lathyrus odoratus* 'Antique Fantasy Mixed')

1 *extra Alchemilla mollis* (replaces *Geranium endressi* 'Wargrave Pink')

3 *Saxifraga × urbicum* (saxifrage) (replace *Aster novi-belgii*)

2 *Digitalis purpurea* 'Excelsior Hybrids' (foxglove) (replace *Althaea rosea*)

2 *Dicentra spectabilis* (replace *Lupinus* 'Russell Hybrids')

3 *Hesperis matronalis* (replace *Delphinium* 'Pacific Hybrids')

1 *Kniphofia uvaria*

HESPERIS (short)

KNIPHOFIA (short)

SAXIFRAGA (short)

DICENTRA (short)

ALCHEMILLA (short)

DIGITALIS (medium)

LATHYRUS (tall)

April Prepare the bed and plant following the instructions on page 52.

In subsequent years, plant new foxglove and campanula each year.

May Support hesperis by pushing pea sticks in between the plants. In windy areas it is also advisable to support dicentra in the same way.

Train the sweet pea plants up on to the trellis or netting they are to grow up. Put a few pea sticks in front of the plants to encourage them to spread outwards across the wall or fence behind them. Once they have started to climb they are entirely self-supporting.

June Deadhead the everlasting sweet peas regularly, snipping off the flower stems, and cut them for the house just as you would with normal sweet peas.

Deadhead saxifrage by cutting the flower stems to ground level after the flowers are over.

July Leave hesperis flower heads to seed.

Deadhead the dicentra by cutting off the flowers, and continue deadheading the everlasting sweet peas.

August Continue deadheading the everlasting sweet peas as above.

September Cut down the dead flower stems and old foliage of alchemilla and dicentra. Remove the old flower stems only of kniphofia.

Pull out foxglove plants after the flowers are finished.

Continue deadheading the everlasting sweet peas.

October Cut down the stems and foliage of everlasting sweet peas to ground level.

1 *Everlasting sweet peas:* June–September
2 *Alchemilla:* June–August **3** *Saxifrage:* May **4** *Foxgloves:* June–July
5 *Dicentra:* May–June **6** *Hesperis:* June
7 *Kniphofia:* July–September
8 *Bourbon rose* **9** *Verbascum*
10 *Geranium* ('Johnson's Blue')
11 *Campanula* **12** *Dianthus*

Border for Cut Flowers

One of the great joys of an old-fashioned border is being able to cut flowers for the house. This variation includes plants for flower arranging, for a garden that gives pleasure indoors and out.

April

12 *Lathyrus odoratus* 'Spencer Mixed' (sweet peas) (replace *Clematis montana*)

4 *Lilium regale* (replace *Verbascum bombyciferum* 'Silver Lining')

1 *Hosta fortunei* 'Albopicta' (replaces *Geranium* 'Johnson's Blue')

3 *Viola* 'Yellow Queen' (pansy) (replace *Geranium* 'Wargrave Pink')

3 *Aster* × *frikartii* (replace *Aster novi-belgii*)

2 *Scabiosa caucasica* 'Clive Greaves' (scabious) (replace *Campanula medium*)

2 *Phlox paniculata* 'Chintz' (replace *Lupinus* 'Russell Hybrids')

1 *Lavandula spica* 'Hidcote' (replaces *Alchemilla mollis*)

4 *Dianthus* 'Doris' (modern pink) (replace *Dianthus* 'Mrs Sinkins')

May

3 *Nicotiana alata* 'Sensation Mixed' (replace *Althaea rosea*)

Tools required

Shears

ASTER (short)

SCABIOUS (short)

DIANTHUS (short)

PHLOX (short)

LAVANDULA (short)

VIOLA (dwarf)

LILIUM (medium)

HOSTA (short)

NICOTIANA (short)

LATHYRUS (tall)

April   Plant the sweet peas, hosta, pansies, aster, scabious, phlox, lavender and dianthus following the instructions on page 52.

Plant the lilies following the instructions on page 58.

> **In subsequent years**, replant the pansies and the sweet peas.

May   Plant out nicotiana after the last danger of frost has passed, following the instructions on page 52.

> **In subsequent years**, replant nicotiana.

Always take a bucket of fresh water with you when you gather flowers, and stand them straight in it immediately they are cut. When you have enough, take them indoors and stand them in a cool shady place for an hour to allow them to take a good drink. When you arrange them, try to cut the stems to the right length under water to prevent air getting into them and put them straight into a vase of fresh water to which cut flower preservative has been added. This will ensure the flowers last as long as possible.

> **In subsequent years**, mulch between the lilies, taking care not to break off any young shoots.

Support aster and phlox with pea sticks.

Put pea sticks in for some of the sweet peas to grow up. Train one row up the trellis or fence at the back of the bed, the second up the pea sticks.

June, July   Protect hostas from slugs by scattering slug pellets round them every 2–3 weeks, especially after rain.

Deadhead pansies and dianthus regularly, snipping off the flower stems, to encourage plenty of new flowers.

August   Continue deadheading pansies, as above, and protecting hostas against slugs.

September   Cut down phlox and hosta to ground level after the foliage has started to die off naturally. Cut down dead flower stems and foliage from the lilies.

Pull out nicotiana, sweet peas and pansies when the last of the flowers are over.

Clip lavender with shears to remove the dead flowers and reshape the plants. Do not cut into the old, dark-coloured wood as this may kill the plant.

> **In subsequent years**, dianthus may need light pruning: cut straggly or broken shoots back to base.

October   Cut down scabious to ground level. Remove all debris from the bed and leave it tidy for winter.

1 *Sweet peas:* June–September
2 *Lilies:* July   3 *Hosta:* July
4 *Pansies:* May–September
5 *Asters:* August–October
6 *Scabious:* June–September
7 *Nicotiana:* June–September
8 *Phlox:* July–September
9 *Lavender:* July–September
10 *Dianthus:* June–July
11 *Bourbon rose*   12 *Delphiniums*

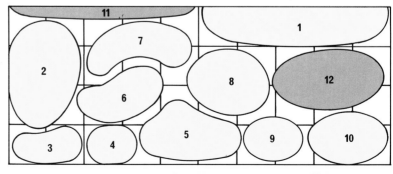

Shady

Not everyone is lucky enough to have a border in a sunny position, so for those who don't the final variation is for an old-fashioned border that will add a dash of colour to a shady spot.

April

1 *Lonicera periclymenum* 'Serotina' (honeysuckle) (replaces *Rosa* 'Madame Isaac Pereire')

1 *Lonicera periclymenum* 'Belgica' (honeysuckle) (replaces *Clematis montana*)

4 *Lilium regale* (lily) (replace *Verbascum bombyciferum* 'Silver Lining')

3 *Viola* 'Swiss Giants' (pansy) (replace *Geranium* 'Johnson's Blue')

1 *Alchemilla mollis* (replaces *Geranium* 'Wargrave Pink')

3 *Pulmonaria officinalis*, and
1 *Heuchera sanguinea* 'Bressingham Blaze' (replace *Aster novi-belgii*)

1 *Helleborus orientalis* (replaces *Campanula medium*)

3 *Digitalis purpurea* 'Excelsior Hybrids' (foxglove) (replace *Althaea rosea*)

1 *Polygonatum multiflorum* (Solomon's seal),
1 *Solidago caesia*, and
3 *Aquilegia* 'McKana Hybrids' (columbine) (replace *Lathyrus odoratus* 'Antique Fantasy Mixed')

2 *Hemerocallis* 'Golden Chimes' (replace *Lupinus* 'Russell Hybrids')

2 *Primula vulgaris* (replace *Alchemilla mollis*)

3 *Anemone* × *hybrida* (replace *Delphinium* 'Pacific Hybrids')

October

4 *Convallaria majalis* (lily of the valley) (replace *Dianthus* 'Mrs Sinkins')

LILIUM (medium)

AQUILEGIA (short)

PULMONARIA (dwarf)

VIOLA (dwarf)

HELLEBORUS (short)

HEUCHERA (short)

LONICERA (tall) 'Belgica'

LONICERA (tall) 'Serotina'

HEMEROCALLIS
(short)

PRIMULA
(dwarf)

ANEMONE (short)

CONVALLARIA (dwarf)

SOLIDAGO (short)

POLYGONATUM (short)

DIGITALIS (medium)

April   To plant the lilies, dig holes
9 inches (23cm) deep and sprinkle a
little compost at the bottom of each. Put
one bulb in each hole, pointed end up,
and settle it into the compost with a
slight twisting motion. Fill in with soil
and firm it down with the handle of the
trowel.

Plant the honeysuckle, pansies,
alchemilla, pulmonaria, heuchera,
helleborus, foxglove, Solomon's seal,
solidago, columbine, hemerocallis,
primula and anemone following the
instructions on page 52.

> **In subsequent years**, replant
> pansies and foxgloves annually.

> **In subsequent years**, prune the honeysuckle if it
> becomes overgrown or straggly. Cut back as
> required to a maximum of 50 per cent of the size of
> the plant, always cutting just above the leaf joints.
> Regular pruning is not necessary. Deadhead the
> hellebore and primula after flowering.
>
> Mulch carefully between the lilies, taking care not
> to break off any of the young shoots just coming
> through.

June   Apply slug pellets regularly.

Deadhead the pansies every two weeks, snipping off the flower stems, to encourage a constant supply of new flowers to develop. Cut back pulmonaria and lily of the valley flower stems after flowering.

Cut columbine flower stems down to ground level, after flowering.

July, August   Continue applying slug pellets, and dead-heading pansies.

September   Pull out pansies and foxgloves after the last flowers are over.

Cut down the flower stems and old leaves of alchemilla.

Cut Solomon's seal down to ground level when the leaves start to die off, and hemerocallis as soon as the flowers are over. Cut down and remove dead flower stems and foliage from the lilies when they start to die back.

Cut off heuchera flower stems after flowering.

Cut down anemone to ground level after flowering is over. Cut solidago flower stems to ground level after flowering.

October   Plant the crowns of lily of the valley, pointed ends uppermost, just below the surface of the soil.

> **In subsequent years**, dig up and divide anemone and Solomon's seal when the clumps become large. Use two garden forks back to back to lever them apart. Replant the best pieces in the same position as previously.

1 *Honeysuckle* ('Serotina'): July–October
2 *Honeysuckle* ('Belgica'): May–June
3 *Lilies:* June
4 *Pansies:* June–September
5 *Alchemilla:* June–August
6 *Pulmonaria:* April–May
7 *Heuchera:* June–September
8 *Helleborus:* February–March
9 *Foxgloves:* June–July
10 *Solomon's seal:* June
11 *Solidago:* August–September
12 *Columbine:* May–June
13 *Hemerocallis:* June–August
14 *Primulas:* April
15 *Lilies of the valley:* April–May
16 *Anemones:* August–October

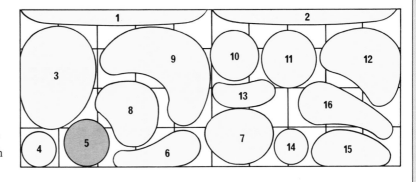

Paved Gardens

A planting scheme to add all-year-round interest and seasonal variation to an area of paving 16ft × 14ft (5m × 4m). The scheme would be perfect for a small town garden or a patio.

Ingredients for a paved garden 16ft × 14ft (5m × 4m)

March

To plant in the paving

1 *Berberis thunbergii* 'Rose Glow'

2 *Alchemilla mollis*

2 *Bergenia* 'Ballawley Hybrids'

6 *Dianthus* 'Doris'

1 *Geranium* 'Johnson's Blue'

6 *Nigella damascena*

1 *Santolina chamaecyparissus*

3 *Armeria maritima* (thrift)

12 *Mixed Godetia*

2 *Saxifraga × urbium* (saxifrage)

To plant in pots

1 *Camellia × Williamsii* 'Donation'

1 *Azalea mollis*

April

To plant in the paving

1 *Euonymus fortunei* 'Emerald 'n' Gold'

1 *Elaeagnus pungens* 'Maculata'

To plant in pots

3 *Agapanthus* 'Headbourne Hybrid'

May

To plant in pots

5 *Begonia semperflorens*

10 *Petunia* 'Resisto Mixed'

1 *Pelargonium* 'Apple Blossom'

6 *Lobelia* (trailing)

5 *Impatiens* 'Pastel Mixed'

September

To plant in the paving

4 *Myosotis alpestris* 'Blue Ball' (forget-me-not)

From the garden shed

Small packet of slug pellets

1 bag of ordinary potting compost

1 bag of potting compost suitable for ericaceous plants

2 × 15 inch (38cm) diameter pots or tubs
2 × 12 inch (30cm) diameter pots
4 × 8 inch (20cm) diameter pots
  all frost resistant, and with drainage holes

Bottle of liquid plant feed

11–22 × 2 gal (10 litre) bucketfuls of peat, well-rotted garden compost or manure

22oz (625g) Growmore fertilizer

Tools required

Spade

Fork

Rake

Hand trowel

Watering can or hose

Secateurs

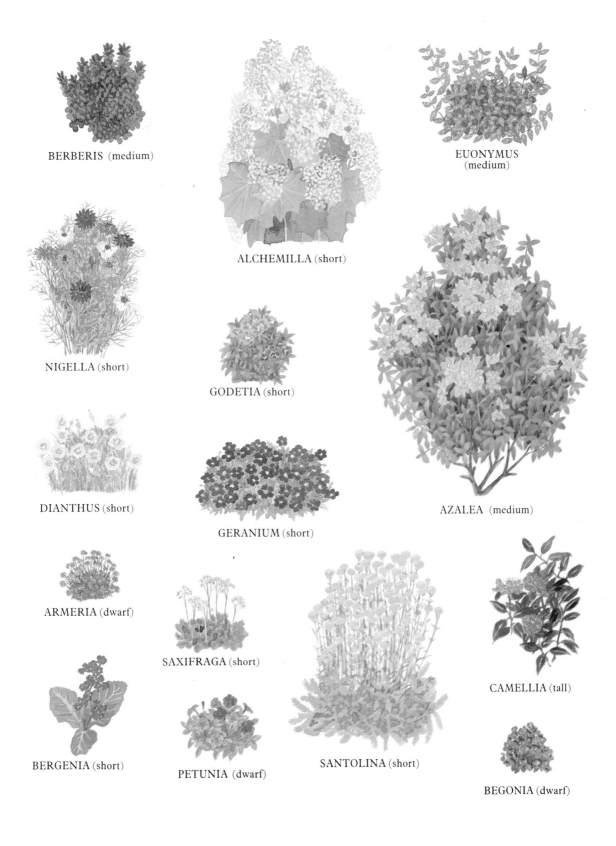

BERBERIS (medium)

ALCHEMILLA (short)

EUONYMUS
(medium)

NIGELLA (short)

GODETIA (short)

DIANTHUS (short)

GERANIUM (short)

AZALEA (medium)

ARMERIA (dwarf)

SAXIFRAGA (short)

CAMELLIA (tall)

BERGENIA (short)

PETUNIA (dwarf)

SANTOLINA (short)

BEGONIA (dwarf)

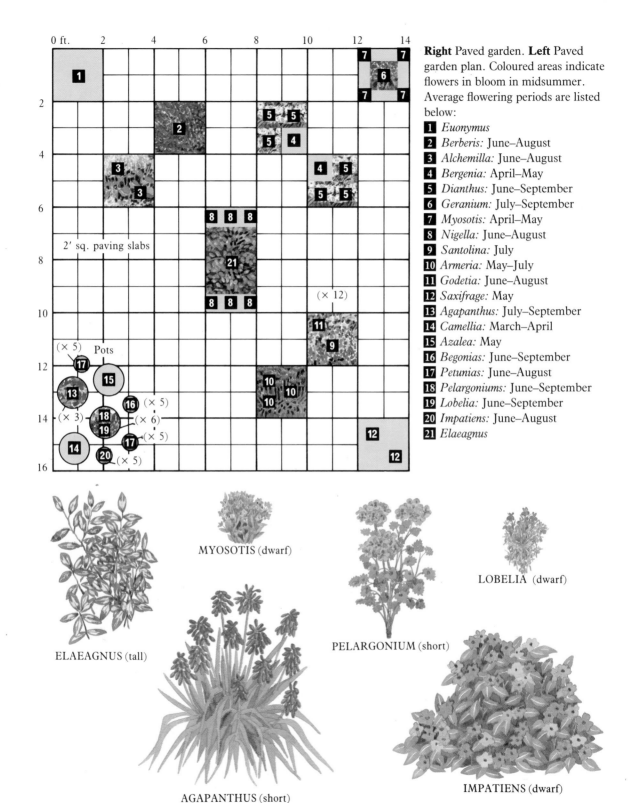

Right Paved garden. **Left** Paved garden plan. Coloured areas indicate flowers in bloom in midsummer. Average flowering periods are listed below:

1 *Euonymus*
2 *Berberis:* June–August
3 *Alchemilla:* June–August
4 *Bergenia:* April–May
5 *Dianthus:* June–September
6 *Geranium:* July–September
7 *Myosotis:* April–May
8 *Nigella:* June–August
9 *Santolina:* July
10 *Armeria:* May–July
11 *Godetia:* June–August
12 *Saxifrage:* May
13 *Agapanthus:* July–September
14 *Camellia:* March–April
15 *Azalea:* May
16 *Begonias:* June–September
17 *Petunias:* June–August
18 *Pelargoniums:* June–September
19 *Lobelia:* June–September
20 *Impatiens:* June–August
21 *Elaeagnus*

2' sq. paving slabs

Pots

ELAEAGNUS (tall)

MYOSOTIS (dwarf)

LOBELIA (dwarf)

PELARGONIUM (short)

AGAPANTHUS (short)

IMPATIENS (dwarf)

Method

If you are starting with an existing paved area, lift and take away paving slabs approximately equivalent to those shown as removed on the plan. If you are laying a new area of paving, simply leave out the appropriate slabs to allow the necessary spaces for planting.

Good soil preparation is very important when planting in spaces between paving slabs. This is because paving is usually laid on to areas of hardcore or builders' rubble, which does not provide much nourishment for plants. Unfortunately, in the limited space between slabs 'normal' soil preparation is not so easy to do. So forget the usual method and instead dig out a $\frac{1}{4}$ bucket of soil from each sq ft (30 × 30 cm) of bed space, remove it entirely, and replace it with peat, compost or manure. Use a garden fork to mix the compost roughly in with the remaining soil. If the soil underneath your paving turns out to consist of a great deal of rubble with very little soil, then increase the amount you remove to $\frac{1}{2}$ bucket from each sq ft (30 × 30 cm), and replace with the same amount of compost.

Sprinkle $\frac{1}{2}$oz (15g) Growmore fertilizer evenly over each sq ft (30 × 30 cm) of the beds that have now been formed amongst the paving slabs, and mix it in with a fork.

March

Planting Plant out the berberis, alchemilla, bergenia, dianthus, geranium, santolina, armeria and saxifrage in the beds.

Place the plants, still in their pots, in the positions they are to be planted in.

Knock each in turn out of its pot, without breaking up the ball of roots inside – tap the base of the pot with the trowel handle to loosen it. Then dig a hole in the planting position the same size as the plant pot. Sit the plant in the hole, and turn its 'best' side to face the direction the plant will most often be seen from. Firm the soil very lightly down round the rootball with the handle of the trowel.

Water plants with hose or watering can. Give the berberis and santolina 1 gal (4.5 litres) of water each, and the alchemilla, bergenia, dianthus, geranium, armeria and saxifrage about 2pts (1 litre) each.

Apply a light scattering of slug pellets evenly round the plants.

To plant the azalea and camellia, first place the containers in position. Half fill each of the two largest with the special potting compost for ericaceous plants.

Stand the azalea in one and the camellia in the other, still in their pots. The rim of each pot should stand about 1 inch (2.5cm) below the top of each container.

Knock the plants carefully out of their pots, without breaking up the ball of root, and stand each one in the centre of its pot. Fill in round the roots with more of the compost, and firm gently down. Water the containers thoroughly, giving each one approximately 3pts (1.7 litres) of water.

To sow the nigella and godetia, rake the soil into a fine tilth. Scatter the seeds over the surface, then rake them lightly until they are covered with soil.

MAINTENANCE

Feed the azalea and camellia twice a week from now until the end of summer.

> **Special note**
> When the roots of a plant have penetrated down into the soil, looking at the condition of the surface is no longer enough. You need to know how moist the soil is further down, so stick your finger or the probe of an electronic water meter in to a depth of 3–4 inches (7.5–10cm). If you are still unsure whether to water or not, dig out a handful of soil and inspect it.

April

Plant the euonymus and elaeagnus in the beds, following the instructions for berberis etc.

Plant the 3 agapanthus in a group in one of the 12 inch (30cm) containers, using the ordinary potting compost. Water thoroughly, giving the container about 3pts (1.7 litres) of water.

Feed the agapanthus twice a week.

If slugs seem plentiful, apply a light scattering of slug pellets, especially round the bergenia.

Feed the azalea and camellia twice a week.

Thin the nigella and godetia seedlings to leave 6 and 12 strong plants respectively, well spaced apart.

May

Plant the begonia, petunia, pelargonium, lobelia and impatiens. Fill the remaining five containers to within 1 inch (2.5cm) of the rim with ordinary potting compost, and make small holes with the trowel just big enough to take the roots of the plants. Firm gently round them, and water after planting.

Continue to feed the agapanthus, azalea and camellia twice a week.

June

Watch out for the very occasional weed that may appear in the beds or containers and pull it out before it gets too big. It is still a lot less weeding than you would need to do in a 'normal' garden. Feed the agapanthus, azalea and camellia twice a week.

July

When the first flush of flowers on the petunia, begonia, pelargonium, lobelia, impatiens and nigella are over, remove the dead heads with secateurs or else nip them off between thumb and forefinger. This keeps the plants looking good, and encourages them to produce lots more flowers. Continue watching out for weeds, and feed the agapanthus, azalea and camellia twice a week.

August

Continue weeding, if necessary, and feed the agapanthus, azalea and camellia twice a week.

September

Plant the forget-me-nots following the instructions for berberis etc.

Pull out and throw away the petunia, begonia, lobelia, impatiens, godetia and nigella after flowering.

Keep the pelargonium if you have a warm greenhouse or a windowsill indoors where it can live for the winter. Dig it out of its container and place in a small plastic pot with a little potting compost round the roots.

Tip out the compost from the vacant containers, clean

(September)

them thoroughly with hot water and a stiff brush, and leave them tidy. If you have space in a shed or garage to store them they can be put right away until next spring.

When the geranium, myosotis, bergenia and alchemilla start to die back naturally, cut their leaves back to ground level and remove any debris.

The dianthus, armeria and saxifrage may need a little light pruning to keep them looking tidy – select straggly or broken shoots and use secateurs to cut the entire shoot right back to its base.

> **In subsequent years**, the elaeagnus, santolina, berberis and euonymus may require light pruning to keep them in shape or repair physical damage; cut out entire shoots back to a main branch to make them look tidy. This way you also avoid leaving untidy 'snags' where plant diseases start up.

October

Reduce the water you give to the plants and stop feeding them.

November

Prepare the plants in containers for winter.

Keep the agapanthus in its container and stand it in a frost-free shed, greenhouse or porch for the winter. The camellia may be left outside, provided your paved garden is reasonably well sheltered from wind and in a part of the country that is not liable to very severe winters. In other areas, it is advisable to stand it, still in its container, inside a frost-free greenhouse or porch for the winter. It must be kept in the light so a shed is unacceptable except as a very temporary measure.

In exceptionally cold districts, the azalea may need to be kept in a greenhouse for winter, but in most places it is sufficient to 'lag' the pot with newspaper, polythene or old sacking to protect the roots from very hard freezing. Ensure the container is not left standing in a puddle of water, if necessary raising it up on some bricks to ensure excess water can drain away from the plant.

Purely Perennial

This low-maintenance scheme uses perennials. Buy the following plants instead of those shown in brackets.

March

To plant in the paving

2 *Hosta fortunei* 'Albopicta' (replace *Berberis thunbergii* 'Rose Glow')

1 *Gypsophila paniculata* 'Bristol Fairy' (replaces *Elaeagnus pungens* 'Maculata')

2 *Campanula lactiflora* (replace *Nigella damascena*)

To plant in pots

1 *Nepeta* × *faassenii* (replaces *Petunia* in first pot)

1 *Helianthemum nummularium* (replaces *Impatiens*)

April

To plant in the paving

4 *Anaphalis triplinervis* (replace *Santolina chamaecyparissus* and *Godetia*)

To plant in pots

1 *Sedum* × 'Autumn Joy' (replaces *Azalea mollis*)

1 *Campanula carpatica* 'Jingle Bells' (replaces *Petunia* in second pot)

3 *Sempervivums* (replace *Begonia semperflorens*)

1 *Yucca filamentosa* (replaces *Pelargonium* 'Apple Blossom' and *Lobelia*)

Tools required

Shears

SEDUM (short)

YUCCA (short)

HOSTA (short)

GYPSOPHILA (medium)

CAMPANULA LACTIFLORA (medium)

SEMPERVIVUM (dwarf)

HELIANTHEMUM (dwarf)

ANAPHALIS (short)

CAMPANULA CARPATICA (dwarf)

March Plant out the hosta, *Campanula lactiflora* and gypsophila, following the planting and watering instructions for the berberis etc on page 70.

Plant the nepeta and helianthemum in pots, following the potting, feeding and watering instructions for begonia etc on page 71.

April Plant the anaphalis, following the planting and watering instructions for the berberis etc on page 70.

Plant the sedum, *Campanula carpatica*, sempervivums and yucca, following the potting, feeding and watering instructions for begonia etc on page 71.

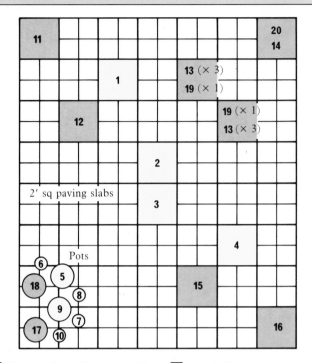

2′ sq paving slabs

Pots

1 *Hostas*   **2** *Gypsophila:* June–August   **3** *Campanula lactiflora:* June–July   **4** *Anaphalis:* August
5 *Sedum:* September–October   **6** *Nepeta:* May–September   **7** *Campanula carpatica:* July–August
8 *Sempervivums*   **9** *Yucca*   **10** *Helianthemum:* June–July   **11** *Euonymus*   **12** *Alchemilla*   **13** *Dianthus*
14 *Myosotis*   **15** *Armeria*   **16** *Saxifrage*   **17** *Camellia*   **18** *Agapanthus*   **19** *Bergenia*   **20** *Geranium*

NEPETA (short)

July Cut back the helianthemum with shears after flowering to encourage further flowering.

August Remove flower stems of *Campanula lactiflora*, after flowering.

September When the foliage of sedum and *Campanula carpatica* starts to die back naturally, cut them down level with the top of the pots. Cut flower stems and leaves of hostas and gypsophila to ground level.

October If the anaphalis has become untidy, cut it back hard. Cut back the nepeta. Leave the dead stems on the sedum until spring.

Throughout the winter, protect the yucca and helianthemum from being 'burned' by strong winds: move the pots to a more sheltered place and lag all pots as described on page 72. In the case of the yucca and helianthemum, gather the leaves together into a sheaf and wrap loosely round with paper or fabric tied roughly in place. Uncover the plants when weather permits.

Check that the pots are not standing in water.

Mainly Evergreen

In this variation mainly evergreen plants provide a permanent backdrop of blue, gold, green and red foliage against which seasonal highlights are picked out with colourful annuals. Again, it requires only very little maintenance.

You will not have to buy berberis, bergenia, dianthus, geranium, myosotis, armeria, godetia or saxifrage and will need only 3 nigella instead of 6. All the plants in pots remain as in the main plan.

March

1 *Gypsophila paniculata* 'Bristol Fairy'

April

1 *Chamaecyparis pisifera* 'Boulevard'

1 *Lonicera nitida* 'Baggesen's Gold' (honeysuckle)

3 *Juniperus squamata* 'Blue Star'

1 *Phormium tenax* 'Purpureum'

1 *Juniperus horizontalis*

1 *Chamaecyparis pisifera* 'Filifera Aurea'

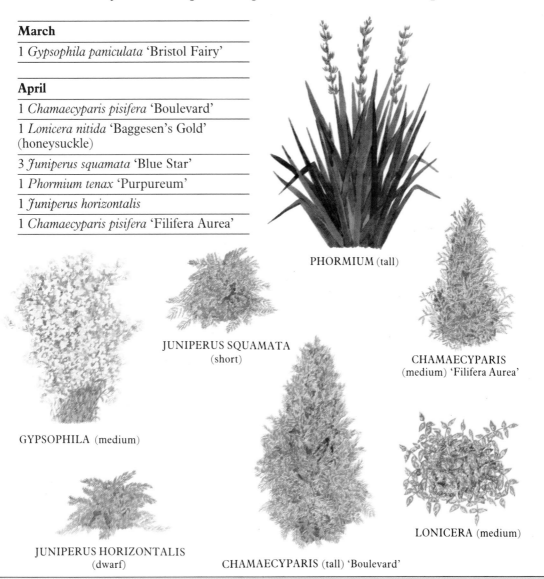

PHORMIUM (tall)

JUNIPERUS SQUAMATA (short)

CHAMAECYPARIS (medium) 'Filifera Aurea'

GYPSOPHILA (medium)

LONICERA (medium)

JUNIPERUS HORIZONTALIS (dwarf)

CHAMAECYPARIS (tall) 'Boulevard'

March Plant the gypsophila following the instructions for berberis etc on page 70.

April Plant the chamaecyparis, honeysuckle, juniper and phormium following the instructions for berberis etc on page 70.

> Replacement and additional plants are given at the start of each variation. For quantities of 'original' plants, uncoloured in the planting plan and not given in the variation ingredients, check with the list at the start of the main plan.

> **In subsequent years**, mulch the honeysuckle with leaf mould or well-rotted compost. If the junipers or chamaecyparis have broken or awkwardly shaped branches cut them back to a main branch or the stem using secateurs. Avoid snipping off odd bits as this can leave the plant open to disease.

June, July Pay particular attention to watering as newly planted evergreens, particularly conifers, are very susceptible to browning foliage if they are allowed to get too dry. Remember that plants growing in paving will not be able to benefit from rainfall as much as those growing in a border.

August Remove dead flower stems from the phormium.

October Cut down the gypsophila. Prune the honeysuckle, removing whole branches rather than a lot of twigs.

December Protect the phormium from frost with straw or bracken.

1 *Gypsophila:* June–August
2 *Chamaecyparis* ('Boulevard')
3 *Honeysuckle:* April–May   **4** *Juniperus squamata*   **5** *Phormium*   **6** *Juniperus horizontalis*   **7** *Chaemacyparis* ('Filifera Aurea')   **8** *Elaeagnus*   **9** *Alchemilla*
10 *Santolina*   **11** *Nigella*   **12** *Euonymus*
13 *Azalea*   **14** *Camellia*   **15** *Agapanthus*
16 *Begonia*   **17** *Petunias*   **18** *Pelargonium*
19 *Lobelia*   **20** *Impatiens*

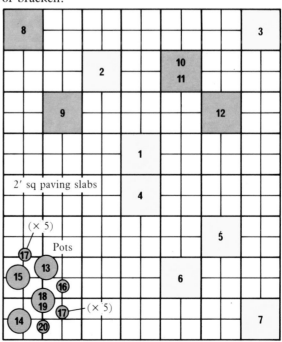

Introducing Bulbs

This variation, the only one in the book which requires autumn planting, introduces spring colour. The ingredients are the same as for the main plan, with the following bulbs:

September

To plant in the paving

12 *Scilla sibirica*

24 *Galanthus nivalis* (snowdrops)

12 *Chionodoxa luciliae*

12 *Narcissus* 'Cheerfulness'

24 *Anemone blanda* ('Mixed')

12 *Muscari armeniacum*

12 *Galtonia candicans*

To plant in pots

6 *Narcissus* 'Jonquil'

6 *Iris unguicularis*

6 *Iris reticulata*

6 *Narcissus triandrus albus*

6 *Narcissus* 'Cheerfulness'

November

To plant in the paving

24 *Tulipa fosteriana* 'Cantata'

From the garden shed

2 × 2 gal (10 litre) bucketfuls of peat, well-rotted compost or manure (for poor soil only)

1 bag of potting compost

NARCISSUS
'Cheerfulness'
(short)

NARCISSUS
'Jonquil'
(short)

NARCISSUS
'Albus'
(short)

TULIPA
(short)

IRIS RETICULATA
(dwarf)

ANEMONE (dwarf)

GALANTHUS
(dwarf)

IRIS UNGUICULARIS
(dwarf)

MUSCARI (dwarf)

CHIONODOXA (dwarf)

SCILLA (dwarf)

September Plant the narcissus 'Cheerfulness', scilla, snowdrops, chionodoxa, anemone and muscari in the beds which contain berberis etc (see plan). Group them in natural-looking clumps among the plants.

Move to the remaining beds and space the bulbs all over the area to create a 'carpet' of colour.

Use a small trowel and scoop out a hole 4 inches (10cm) deep for small bulbs such as snowdrops, scilla and muscari, and 6 inches (15cm) deep for larger bulbs like narcissi. (Note that this is slightly deeper than is sometimes recommended, since these bulbs will be in place permanently.)

Press each bulb down firmly into the bottom of the hole, pointed end up, with a slight screwing motion. This makes sure the base of the bulb is in firm contact with the soil, which will help it root in. If the soil is very poor, dig a hole 2 inches (5cm) deeper before planting and place a handful of peat or well-rotted compost under each bulb. Now replace the soil round and over the bulb, and continue until all are planted. There is no need to water bulbs in after planting.

To plant bulbs in the pots, half fill with fresh potting compost. Plant the iris and narcissi bulbs, one variety per container, saving the larger narcissus 'Cheerfulness' for the biggest container. Press each bulb in turn well down into the compost, and then fill the container to within 1 inch (2.5cm) of the rim with more compost. Water in very lightly – just enough to moisten the compost thoroughly. Provided you have bought large bulbs, they should all flower the following spring.

November Plant the tulip bulbs 6 inches (15 cm) deep following the instructions for scilla etc.

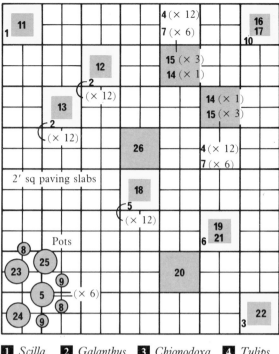

1 Scilla   **2** Galanthus   **3** Chionodoxa   **4** Tulips
5 Narcissus ('Cheerfulness')   **6** Anemones
7 Muscari   **8** Narcissus   **9** Iris
10 Galtonia   **11** Euonymus   **12** Berberis
13 Alchemilla   **14** Bergenia   **15** Dianthus
16 Geranium   **17** Myosotis   **18** Nigella   **19** Santolina
20 Armeria   **21** Godetia   **22** Saxifrage   **23** Agapanthus
24 Camellia   **25** Azalea   **26** Elaeagnus

The following March, after flowering, nip the dead heads off but do not cut the foliage back or tie it in knots, as is often done. Instead let it die back naturally, and when it is completely yellow or brown cut it off at ground level and clear it away. Bulbs growing in containers may be dug out and replanted elsewhere after flowering – there is no need to wait until the foliage dies back if you do it carefully and avoid damaging the roots. Mark the spot where you plant them, and you can dig the same bulbs up again next August to replant in the original containers. In the meantime, the same set of containers can be used for summer bedding plants.

With Herbs

This variation introduces a cottage flavour – not to mention scent – to the basic theme, using a mixture of decorative and ornamental herbs. Buy the following plants instead of those shown in brackets.

March

To plant in the paving

2 *Lavandula spica* 'Hidcote' (lavender) (replace *Bergenia* 'Ballawley Hybrid'

1 *Rosmarinus officinalis* 'Jessop's Upright' (rosemary) (replaces *Geranium* 'Johnson's Blue')

1 *Angelica archangelica* (angelica) (replaces *Saxifraga × urbium*)

May

To plant in the paving

2 *Salvia officinalis* 'Purpurea' (sage) (replace *Elaeagnus pungens* 'Maculata')

4 *Origanum vulgare* 'Aureum' (golden marjoram), and
2 *Allium schoenoprasum* (chives) (replace *Armeria maritima*)

To plant in pots

5 *Peucedanum graveolens* (dill) (replace *Azalea mollis*)

5 *Petroselinum crispum* (parsley) (replace *Pelargonium* 'Apple Blossom' and *Lobelia*)

From the garden shed

1 bag ordinary potting compost

ALLIUM (dwarf)

ORIGANUM (dwarf)

PEUCEDANUM (short)

SALVIA (short)

PETROSELINUM (short)

LAVANDULA (short)

ANGELICA (tall)

ROSMARINUS (medium)

March   Plant out the lavender, rosemary and angelica, following the instructions for berberis etc on page 70.

May   Plant out the dill, parsley, marjoram, sage and chives following the instructions for begonia etc on page 71.

> **In subsequent years**, replant dill and parsley.

September   Pull out the parsley and dill and throw them away. Cut down the chives and marjoram as they die back for winter.

   Prune the rosemary and sage slightly, to help them retain their shape. Use sharp secateurs, and simply cut out any broken or untidy branches right back to a main branch. Cut back the lavender lightly, with shears.

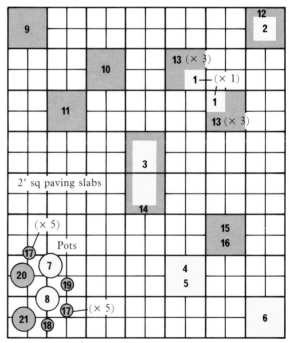

1 *Lavender*   **2** *Rosemary*   **3** *Sage*   **4** *Marjoram*
5 *Chives*   **6** *Angelica*   **7** *Dill*   **8** *Parsley*   **9** *Euonymus*
10 *Berberis*   **11** *Alchemilla*   **12** *Myosotis*   **13** *Dianthus*
14 *Nigella*   **15** *Santolina*   **16** *Godetia*   **17** *Petunias*
18 *Impatiens*   **19** *Begonias*   **20** *Agapanthus*   **21** *Camellia*

Rose Gardens

A formal rose bed has a time-honoured place in the English garden, and the main plan creates a traditional display. A few subtle variations introduce a series of new ideas to the classic rose garden theme.

October or March are the best times to plant a new rose garden, although as 'second best' you can plant any time during the spring and summer provided you only use container-grown roses. Never try to transplant roses dug up from another garden bed between April and September when the plants are growing.

Ingredients for a rose bed 10ft × 5ft (3m × 1.5m)

March

3 Floribunda 'Allgold'

3 Floribunda 'Pink Parfait'

2 Hybrid tea 'Chicago Peace'

2 Miniature 'Baby Masquerade'

2 Miniature 'Baby Darling'

From the garden shed

Rose fungicide

Systemic plant pesticide

Small hand sprayer

Packet rose feed

11 × 2 gal (10 litre) bucketfuls well-rotted horse manure for top dressing

Tools required

Spade

Fork

Rake

Garden line

Hand trowel

Watering can or hose

Secateurs

FLORIBUNDA
(medium) 'Allgold'

MINIATURE
(dwarf)
'Baby Darling'

HYBRID TEA
(tall)

MINIATURE
(dwarf)
'Baby Masquerade'

FLORIBUNDA
(medium)'Pink Parfait'

Method

Choose a sunny situation and mark out an area 10ft × 5ft (3m × 1.5m) with a garden line or four canes and a ball of string. The bed is best cut into a lawn. To keep the formality of the scheme, be sure to line it up so that it runs parallel with any straight feature already in the garden, such as the boundary fence or wall, a path or the edge of a patio. Prepare the soil as described in the introduction.

March

'Bare root' roses (i.e. roses which have not been grown in containers but have been dug up from a bed and sold with their roots wrapped in polythene or other material) are planted now.

Before planting Soak the roots in a bucket of tepid water for an hour. After taking the plants out, use secateurs to carefully trim away any dead or broken bits of root to avoid infections starting in them. At the same time, shorten any roots that are noticeably longer than the others. This makes it easier to plant them properly, and does not harm them in the least.

Now prune the top of the plants, if the nurseryman has not already done this. Cut all of the stems of the hybrid tea roses back to within 4 inches (10cm) of the point where they originate from the main stem, and those of the floribundas to 6 inches (15cm). Prune the miniature roses back to remove about half their height. In each case, cut just above a leaf joint, though it can sometimes be a little difficult to tell exactly where they are if the stems have lost their leaves.

MAINTENANCE

In subsequent years, prune the roses, using sharp secateurs and cutting any dead or thin, weak shoots out entirely, right back to the base. Then cut all the stems of the hybrid tea roses down to about 6 inches (15cm) above ground level, and all the stems of the floribundas down to 8 inches (20cm). Miniature roses need hardly any pruning – just cut them back by about half their height. In all cases, cut neatly just above a leaf as it is from this point that the new shoots will grow.

Feed after pruning, using proprietary rose feed at the rate recommended by the manufacturer. Next give the soil a light cultivation to aerate it. You can use the points of a garden fork to loosen the soil, but do not actually dig it or you may damage the roots of the plants. Alternatively, hoe thoroughly. Spread a mulch of well-rotted horse manure over the whole bed or, if you are using a residual weedkiller, this can be applied instead.

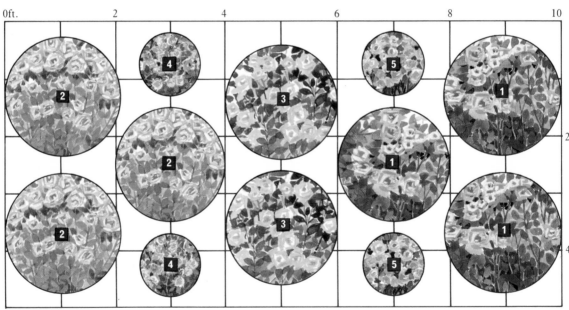

Top Rose garden. **Above** Rose garden plan. Coloured areas indicate roses in bloom in midsummer. Average flowering periods are listed below: **1** *Floribunda* 'Pink Parfait': June–July, September–October **2** *Floribunda* 'Allgold': June–July, September–October **3** *Hybrid tea* 'Chicago Peace': June–October **4** *Miniature* 'Baby Masquerade': June–July, September–October **5** *Miniature* 'Baby Darling': June–July, September–October

(March)

Planting To plant 'bare root' roses, dig a hole rather bigger than the maximum root spread of your rose. Look for the mark on the stem which shows the previous soil level and aim to plant to the same depth again.

Fork over the bottom of the hole to loosen the soil. Stand the plant in the hole and spread the roots out over the bottom of it so they are as far apart as possible. Now place a couple of trowelfuls of soil over the roots to anchor them in place. Very gently firm the soil down with your foot. Fill in the rest of the hole with soil.

Now check to see that the soil mark on the stem matches up with the new level of soil around it. If the plant is too far out of the ground, dig it up and start again. If it is slightly too deep, hold it by the main stem and gently jiggle it about in the soil until you raise it up to the correct level. When the level is correct, firm the soil lightly down all round the plant with your foot.

If you are planting container-grown roses, prune as described for bare root roses. Then simply knock the plant out of its container (give the bottom a sharp tap with the handle of the trowel to loosen it first). The container should fit snugly into the hole, its rim level with the soil surface. Remove it and fork over the bottom of the hole to loosen the soil.

Just before planting, check the condition of the rootball. If the base is just a tight mass of thickly coiled roots, gently tease a few of these out. Then stand the plant in the hole and fill in round the roots with soil. Firm the soil down gently round the rootball with your foot.

It is best to wait a year before cutting roses for the house. The bushes will be well established and producing more flowers than they did in the first year. Avoid taking too many flowers from any one bush at a time and just cut one or two from each instead.

When cutting roses, always take a bucketful of fresh water with you. Use sharp secateurs and cut the stems off cleanly just above a leaf, as if you were pruning. Strip the leaves and thorns from the lower third to half of each cut stem and stand them straight in the bucket of water.

When you have cut enough, take the flowers indoors and keep them in a cool place for an hour before you arrange them. Try to cut the stems to the right length under water and put them into a vase filled with fresh water to which a cut flower preservative has been added. This will ensure they last as long as possible.

(**March**)

Water in the roses, giving each plant about $\frac{1}{2}$ gal (2 litres) of water. If the soil is very dry give the entire bed a thorough soaking, using the hose with your finger partly covering the end of it to produce a fine spray.

Follow up by top dressing the ground between the plants with a layer of well-rotted horse manure.

To plant container-grown roses during summer follow instructions for planting container-grown roses in March, but do not prune.

May

Check newly planted roses regularly every week to see if they need watering. Dig out a handful of soil to the full depth of the trowel to see if it looks or feels dry. If it does, then water thoroughly.

A traditional rose garden like this which has bare soil between the plants needs weeding every week. Any weeds, even small ones, will quickly spoil the appearance of the bed. A hoe is the easiest way of keeping on top of the fast-growing annual weeds which appear quickly in wet weather. The top dressing of manure which was spread over the bed after planting will suppress such weeds to some extent.

June, July, August

Water new roses whenever the soil becomes very dry.

Feed regularly, using a proprietary brand of rose fertilizer and following the manufacturer's instructions. Roses need regular feeding.

Deadhead the flowers as soon as the first flush is over and make it a weekly routine from then on as this will encourage more flowers to bloom. When deadheading, use secateurs and cut off the old flower heads a short way down the stem, just above a healthy green leaf. It is from here that the new shoot will grow.

Examine the plants every week or two to see if they have become infested with aphids, generally found living in colonies towards the top of the plant on young shoots, flower buds and the undersides of young leaves. Although they are commonly called greenfly, aphids may also be pink, brown or even cream in colour. Twisted and contorted leaves are one unpleasant side-effect they pro-

(June, July, August)

Special note

When mixing pesticides follow the manufacturer's instructions carefully. Use a small hand sprayer and mix the pesticide in it to avoid getting any on your hands. Spray in the early morning or evening, when the weather is cool and the sun is not shining on to the plants. Also avoid windy weather, when the spray will be blown away before reaching its objectives. Spray the whole of each plant as thoroughly as possible until the spray just starts to drip off the leaves. Try to cover each leaf on both sides and get the spray well down into the centre of each plant besides spraying the easy bits round the edges. When you have finished spraying, tip any left-over spray away into a hole in the ground, not down the sink or a drain. Once diluted, garden chemicals should not be kept to use later.

duce; another is a nasty black sticky goo that eventually covers the plants. Unfortunately this can only be removed by wiping each leaf individually, front and back, and unless the aphids causing it are killed it will soon return. A few aphids are unlikely to do very much harm, but if numbers increase then you should certainly get rid of them.

Spray every two weeks with any good general systemic plant pesticide.

It is also advisable to spray regularly against blackspot, another common problem of roses. Affected plants produce characteristic black marks on their leaves which spoil their appearance. To keep your plants free of these you will need to spray with a special rose fungicide every two weeks (or as directed by the manufacturers). Unfortunately, spraying will not undo the damage to the leaves but will stop it getting any worse.

Watch out for weeds, which will be starting to grow on top of the manure layer.

Remove any suckers from the roses as soon as they appear. These are very strong, fast-growing shoots that appear from below ground level around the plant and they will rapidly overrun the rose, unless you remove them. Do not cut them off with secateurs, as this just makes them worse. Take a fork and dig down near the rose until you find where the sucker grows out from a root. Then tear it out, so you remove a tiny 'heel' of the root with it. In this way it will not be able to grow back again. Fill in the hole and replace the top dressing of manure over the area.

September

Check for the first signs of mildew. This appears as a powdery substance over some of the leaves, stems and flower buds; as it gets worse it may cover large areas of the plant and some of the leaves may even be shed. Mildew can be especially troublesome in cool, humid weather. Spray with the general rose fungicide that you used during the summer to prevent blackspot. Repeat every two weeks until the end of the autumn.

October

Prune the roses lightly. All that is necessary is to shorten their stems by about half to prevent windrock. Do not bother about cutting neatly just above a leaf-joint as is normally done – a rough cut about halfway up each stem is all that is needed for floribundas and hybrid tea roses. Do not prune the miniatures. Remove the prunings, weed and leave the bed tidy ready for winter.

With Ground Cover Plants

In the original plan, the roses are surrounded by bare soil; in this variation evergreen ground cover plants provide a permanent background to the flowers and also supply interest of their own outside the normal rose season. Once established, they cut down on a lot of the routine weeding, too! They will cover the ground entirely and weeds will not be able to grow through the carpet of foliage covering the bed. If a perennial weed occasionally manages to push through, paint it with Glyphosate gel. For this variation you do not need the Miniature roses 'Baby Masquerade' and 'Baby Darling'.

April

16 *Lamium galeobdelon* 'Beacon Silver'

12 *Iberis sempervirens* (evergreen candytuft)

From the garden shed

About 30 × 8 inch (20cm) lengths of flexible
wire

LAMIUM (dwarf)

IBERIS (dwarf)

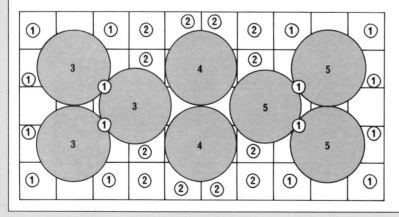

1 *Lamium*: June–July
2 *Iberis*: May–June
3 *Floribunda* 'Allgold'
4 *Hybrid tea* 'Chicago Peace'
5 *Floribunda* 'Pink Parfait'

April Plant the lamium and iberis. Knock them out of their containers by giving the base a sharp tap with the handle of the trowel. Dig the holes exactly the same size as the containers, and fork over the bottom of each hole. Tease a few of the roots free of the rootball and stand the plants in the holes. Fill round the roots with soil, and firm down with your foot.

May Begin to peg the runners of lamium down to the soil, encouraging them to run in all directions. Hold the runners down with wire pegs made by bending 8 inch (20cm) lengths of wire in half to make 'hairpins', and pushing them into the ground either side of a shoot. The pieces pegged down will root and become new plants.

June Continue pegging down lamium shoots.

Feed the entire bed with rose fertilizer (see page 86) washing the granules off the leaves of the lamium and iberis with a hose afterwards.

Remove the developing flower spikes from the lamium.

Weed or hoe carefully between the plants. Alternatively, you can use a weedkiller intended for flowers – those intended for use among shrubs are not usually suitable to use with ground cover plants. Be careful not to exceed the stated dose or it may inhibit the growth of the plants.

July Snip off the dead flower heads from the iberis.

Continue pegging down the lamium shoots, and feeding the bed with fertilizer. Continue weeding or hoeing.

August Continue weeding, as above.

October Stand on the grass round the bed to prune the roses. Avoid walking on the soil.

Replacement and additional plants are given at the start of each variation. For quantities of 'original' plants, uncoloured in the planting plan and not given in the variation ingredients, check with the list at the start of the main plan.

In subsequent years, in **March**, hoe where possible between the lamium and iberis to loosen the soil, but take care not to chop through their stems. As far as you are able, top dress between the plants with a mulch of well-rotted horse manure.

With Dwarf Shrubs

This variation creates an informal border where roses are teamed with dwarf shrubs for a charming cottage effect. You do not need Floribunda 'Allgold', Floribunda 'Pink Parfait' or Miniature 'Baby Masquerade'.

March

1 Miniature 'Baby Darling' (replaces 2)

2 Prostrate rose 'Nozomi'

From the garden shed

About 2½yd (3m) flexible wire to cut into 8 inch (20cm) lengths

April

2 *Salvia officinalis* 'Purpurea'

3 *Santolina chamaecyparissus*

3 *Lavandula spica* 'Hidcote' (lavender)

PROSTRATE ROSE
(dwarf)

LAVANDULA (short)

SANTOLINA (short)

SALVIA (short)

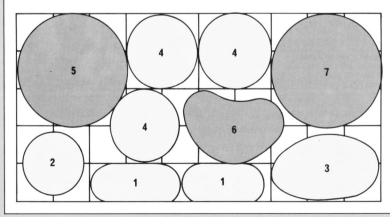

1 *Prostrate rose* 'Nozomi': June–October **2** *Salvia*
3 *Santolina*: July **4** *Lavender*: July–September **5** *Hybrid tea* 'Chicago Peace' **6** *Miniature* 'Baby Darling' **7** *Floribunda* 'Pink Parfait'

March   Plant the prostrate rose 'Nozomi' following the method described on page 85, but do not prune it.

April   Plant the salvia, santolina and lavender. Knock them out of their pots by giving the base a sharp tap with the handle of the trowel. Dig holes the same size as the containers and loosen the soil at the bottom of the hole with a fork. Tease the roots out a little from the rootballs and place the plants into the holes, firming the soil down gently.

> **In subsequent years**, remove any shoots of 'Nozomi' which have grown untidy or have died. 'Nozomi' does not require pruning like normal roses.

June   Start feeding the beds regularly. This is especially important as the shrubs will be competing for the same feed needed by the roses. Wash down the shrubs with the hose after feeding to remove any granules of fertilizer that have become lodged in the foliage. This could otherwise scorch the leaves and spoil their appearance.

July   Remove the flowers of the santolina if you prefer. They are not especially attractive, and in this scheme the plant is used for its decorative silver foliage rather than its flowers.

Remove the dead flower heads of 'Nozomi' when deadheading the other roses (see page 86). Peg its stems down to the ground with pieces of bent wire to hold them in place. The plant should in time form a low mound, and may require slight encouragement to form a nice shape.

August   Continue deadheading 'Nozomi' with the other roses.

September   Clip the lavender and santolina with shears to remove the dead flower heads and to reshape the plants generally.

> **In subsequent years**, clip back lavender, santolina and salvia if they become overgrown, but do not cut them hard back. Lavender especially must not be cut back to old wood (which is darker in colour) as it may die rather than produce any new shoots; use shears.

October   Prune the roses as described on page 87, except for 'Nozomi', which needs no pruning.

> **Special note**
> The main purpose of pruning is to maintain a good shape and to remove any weak or dead shoots. To check whether a shoot is dead or not, look at the inside of it. If it is dead it will be a dull brown colour, while a live, healthy shoot will be a green or creamy colour inside. When you are removing dead shoots, cut back cleanly to just above a live bud so that there is no dead wood left to encourage further die-back.

Fragrant

Fragrance is one of the main attractions of a real old-fashioned rose garden, but one in which many of the newer varieties of rose are unfortunately lacking. This variation brings together some of the most attractively perfumed varieties to create a sweetly scented rose garden.

March

3 Floribunda 'English Miss' (replace floribunda 'Allgold')

3 Floribunda 'Chanelle' (replace floribunda 'Pink Parfait')

2 Hybrid tea 'Alec's Red' (replace hybrid tea 'Chicago Peace')

4 Miniature 'Sweet Fairy' (replace miniature 'Baby Masquerade' and miniature 'Baby Darling')

MINIATURE
(dwarf)

FLORIBUNDA
(medium) 'Chanelle'

FLORIBUNDA
(medium)
'English Miss'

March Prepare the bed and plant as on pages 83 and 85, substituting the roses listed here for those in the original plan. Their subsequent care is exactly as described on pages 86 and 87.

HYBRID TEA (medium)

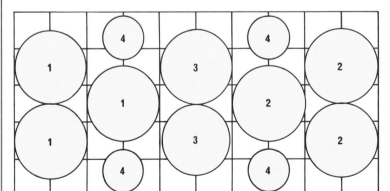

1 *Floribunda* 'English Miss': June–July, September–October
2 *Floribunda* 'Chanelle': June–July, September–October
3 *Hybrid tea* 'Alec's Red': June–October   **4** *Miniature* 'Sweet Fairy': June–July, September–October

With Extra Height

There are many occasions when a little extra height can add variety to a rose bed. In a large garden, or where you want to situate the bed towards the back of an area, height can make all the difference. The final variation introduces standard roses to the original theme without losing its traditional formality. You will not need floribunda 'Pink Parfait'.

March

1 Extra floribunda 'Allgold'

2 Standard trained hybrid tea 'National Trust'

1 *Standard trained hybrid tea* 'National Trust': June–October **2** *Floribunda* 'Allgold' **3** *Miniature* 'Baby Masquerade' **4** *Hybrid tea* 'Chicago Peace' **5** *Miniature* 'Baby Darling'

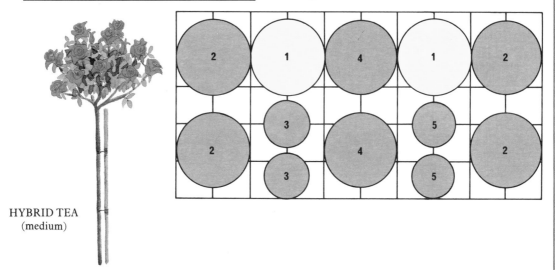

HYBRID TEA
(medium)

March

Prepare the ground and plant the roses as on pages 83 and 85. Prune the standard roses by cutting the stems forming the head of the plant back to within 4 inches (10cm) of the point where they originate from the trunk.

In subsequent years, prune the head of the plant, cutting each shoot back to within 6 inches (15cm) of its point of origin from the trunk. As always, cut just above a leaf joint to avoid the stems dying back.

June, July, August Remove any suckers growing from around the standard roses (see page 87) together with any shoots growing from the trunk so as to keep a clean stem.

October Cut back the stems forming the heads of the standard roses by about half their length.

Conifer Beds

For a truly all-year-round garden, conifers can't be beaten. These striking plants offer a bit of everything – evergreen foliage, eye-catching colours, contrasting textures, a huge range of architectural shapes, even coloured cones – yet require very little maintenance. The variations combine conifers in groups designed to bring out the best of their particular characteristics, while the main plan shows how to make the most of their incredible range of attractions in a small plot.

Ingredients for a bed 15ft × 15ft (4.5m × 4.5m)

April

3 *Chamaecyparis obtusa* 'Nana Gracilis'

3 *Thuja orientalis* 'Aurea Nana'

1 *Abies koreana*

3 *Picea glauca* 'Albertiana Conica'

3 *Juniperus sabina* 'Tamariscifolia'

1 *Chamaecyparis pisifera* 'Boulevard'

From the garden shed

12 × 2 gal (10 litre) bucketfuls of bark chippings, peat, garden compost or manure for mulching (optional)

Plant stakes and tree ties (see 'Maintenance', April)

1 inch (2.5cm) nails

7 × 7ft (2m) poles

30ft (9m) sacking or 5ft (1.5m) wide polythene or anti-transpirant spray

Residual weedkiller (optional)

Tools required

Spade

Fork

Rake

Garden line

Hand trowel

Watering can or hose and lawn sprinkler

Secateurs

Hoe (optional)

THUJA ORIENTALIS
(short)

CHAMAECYPARIS PISIFERA (tall)

Method

Choose a sunny site for conifers, and preferably one that is slightly sheltered from the worst of the winter winds. Mark the bed out with a garden line. It should be cut into a lawn, as the plan is for an island bed. As it is a formal shape, the bed should be aligned to run parallel with any existing straight features in the garden, such as the side of the house, the garden fence or a path. Prepare the soil as described in the introduction.

Conifers are available in containers or, less often, with their roots in a ball of soil wrapped in sacking. Either way, buy strong, healthy plants that are a good green colour right the way down to the pot, with no browning of the lower branches. Choose small plants in preference to large ones; they will become established much faster. Large conifers can be riskier to establish, and are more demanding to look after.

PICEA (medium)

ABIES (tall)

CHAMAECYPARIS OBTUSA (tall)

JUNIPERUS (short)

April

Before planting Give container-grown conifers a thorough watering and let them stand for 12 hours to soak up plenty of moisture. If you are using root-wrapped plants, untie the wrappings and soak the roots in a bucketful of tepid water for an hour before planting. Try not to remove any soil from the roots in the process.

Stand the conifers in their positions on the prepared bed.

Planting To plant container-grown conifers, dig a hole big enough to take the container, leaving its rim level with the surrounding soil. Fork over the soil at the bottom of the hole to loosen it slightly. If the plant is in a rigid pot knock it out, first giving the bottom of the pot a sharp tap with the trowel handle to loosen it. If it is of the black plastic bag type, cut it away, taking care not to slice into the rootball.

Check the base of the rootball; if it is a mass of tightly coiled roots, gently tease a few of these out. This will help the plant to get established and grow better, since the roots will be able to find their way out into the surrounding soil faster.

Stand the plant in the hole. Turn it so that its best side faces the outside of the bed and fill in round the roots with soil. Finally, firm down gently round the rootball with your foot.

To plant root-wrapped conifers, dig a hole slightly wider than the rootball and about the same depth. It is important not to make the hole too deep; the idea is to replant at the same depth the conifer was growing at the nursery. Look for the mark on the stem which shows where the soil came to previously, and aim to have this correspond to the new soil level.

MAINTENANCE

Stake any particularly tall conifers to support them while they become established. Take a strong plant stake 18 inches (46cm) longer than the height of the plant and hammer it into the ground about 4–6 inches (10–15cm) away from the trunk, taking care not to damage the rootball.

Use proper tree ties to secure the trunk to the stake.

Protect newly planted conifers from the wind after planting. This is very important, as otherwise they can very quickly turn brown. Once they have done so they do not generally recover unless the damage is only slight.

There are two ways to protect conifers from windy weather. The first is to put up a temporary screen of sacking or polythene round the whole bed. This calls for a support structure sturdy enough to hold the windbreak steady even in strongish winds. Seven 7ft (2m) poles with a point at one end hammered in 18 inches (46cm) deep round the windward side of the bed, at 5ft (1.5m) intervals, will suffice. Nail the sacking or plastic to them, stretching it tightly between adjacent posts.

The other, less obtrusive, way of protecting conifers from 'wind-burn' is to use an anti-transpirant product. Spray this thoroughly all over each plant, following the manufacturer's instructions, and it should protect them for about 2 weeks. Repeat the application if necessary.

Mulch between the plants, if required, with a layer of bark chippings, peat or well-rotted manure or garden compost.

The following year, feed by scattering Growmore evenly over the soil between the plants at the rate of 2oz (50g) per sq yd (sq m). Hoe this lightly in, and follow with a thorough watering if it does not rain within 2–3 days. Wash any granules of fertilizer off the plants with a hose if they lodge in the foliage, or it may be scorched.

Mulch the entire conifer bed with a new dressing of peat, well-rotted manure or compost to 'top up' what is left of last year's material. Be sure the soil is moist before mulching. Alternatively, hoe the bed to remove weeds and then apply a new application of residual weedkiller.

Remove any stakes that were provided to support tall conifers. The plants should be well established.

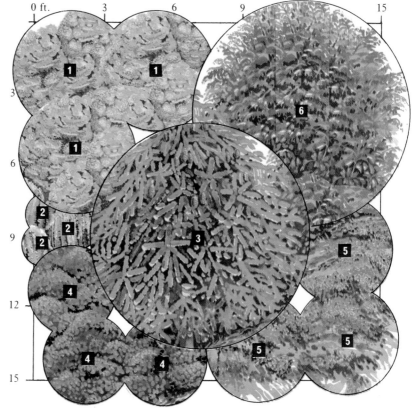

Above Conifer bed.
Right Conifer bed plan.
1 *Chamaecyparis obtusa*
2 *Thuja* **3** *Abies*
4 *Picea* **5** *Juniperus*
6 *Chamaecyparis pisifera*

(April)

Fork over the bottom of the hole to loosen the soil and, without breaking the rootball up, stand the plant in it. Now check to see that the soil mark on the stem matches up with the new level of soil around it. If the plant is too high or low in the ground, dig it up and start again. When the level is correct, fill in round the rootball with soil and firm down all round the plant with your foot.

Water the conifers in, giving each plant about ½ gal (2 litres) of water.

> **In subsequent years**, clip picea very lightly with hedging shears to give the plants a good conical shape just before they put on their burst of growth. Needles cut in half by clipping will then soon disappear under the new layer of growth.
>
> Prune conifers that are growing out of shape just to restore their appearance.

May

> **Special note**
> To use a residual weedkiller first clear the bed of weeds as these products work by preventing new weeds from germinating; they do not kill existing ones. Then scatter the granules over the surface of the bed, following the manufacturer's instructions, and use a hose to dislodge any granules left behind on the plants. Water the weedkiller in if it does not rain within 24 hours, or as directed.
>
> Avoid disturbing the soil surface thereafter.

Hoe or hand weed regularly every week if mulching was not done to ensure new plants do not become smothered by weeds.

Water newly planted conifers whenever the soil is dry, as they turn brown if they lack moisture. Usually the base of the plant turns brown first, but in very dry conditions the whole plant can go brown.

The best way to avoid this happening is to check the soil every week by digging down to the depth of a trowel and feeling if the soil is moist at that level.

> **The following year**, make sure you keep the conifers well watered in dry spells to enable them to make the most of their maximum growth period.
>
> **In subsequent years**, the plants will spread to cover the ground in the bed. You can then discontinue mulching or applying weedkiller; the shade cast by the plants will prevent weeds from germinating.

June, July, August

Continue to weed and water regularly during the summer.

September

Pruning is not generally needed as the type of conifers used in this scheme are slow growing. If, however, a branch happens to become broken or grow out of shape, it is best to cut it right back to its junction with a main branch. Avoid snipping little bits here and there, or leaving short stumps which can often become infected with plant diseases later. Now is a good time to do this job as conifers may undergo a second short flush of growth later this month, and you should ideally do any pruning or trimming just before it starts.

Gold

Gold foliage is used in various shades to create a bed with a distinctive and bright appearance. For the plants in the original plan, substitute the following.

April

30 *Thuja orientalis* 'Aurea Nana'

2 *Chamaecyparis pisifera* 'Filifera Aurea'

16 *Thuja occidentalis* 'Rheingold'

1 *Chamaecyparis obtusa* 'Tetragona Aurea'

From the garden shed

You will also need seaweed fertilizer

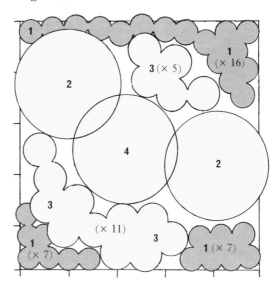

1 *Thuja orientalis*   **2** *Chamaecyparis pisifera*
3 *Thuja occidentalis*   **4** *Chamaecyparis obtusa*

CHAMAECYPARIS PISIFERA (medium)

THUJA (short)

CHAMAECYPARIS OBTUSA (short)

April   Prepare and plant the bed and carry out routine maintenance as described on pages 96 and 98.

In subsequent years, do not feed the bed with Growmore. Instead, apply liquid feeds containing seaweed extract every 2 weeks from late April till the end of May – this will be just before and during the main flush of growth. Seaweed fertilizers seem to bring out the best colours in golden-leaved conifers.

Emphasizing Form

This variation uses plants that demonstrate the architectural characteristics of conifers. You will need the following plants in place of those in the original plan.

April	
8 *Picea glauca* 'Albertiana Conica'	1 *Tsuga canadensis* 'Pendula'
1 *Chamaecyparis lawsoniana* 'Ellwoodii'	2 *Chamaecyparis obtusa* 'Nana Gracilis'
3 *Cedrus libani* 'Sargentii'	2 *Juniperus horizontalis*
	3 *Pinus sylvestris* 'Beuvronensis'

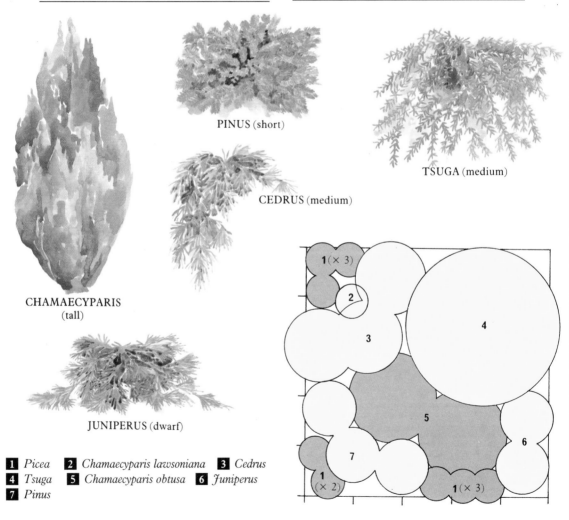

PINUS (short)

TSUGA (medium)

CEDRUS (medium)

CHAMAECYPARIS
(tall)

JUNIPERUS (dwarf)

1 *Picea* **2** *Chamaecyparis lawsoniana* **3** *Cedrus*
4 *Tsuga* **5** *Chamaecyparis obtusa* **6** *Juniperus*
7 *Pinus*

April   Follow the method of planting described on page 96.

Follow the instructions for maintenance given on pages 96 and 98.

Low-Growing

The main plan and both the previous variations included plants which will lend height to the bed to create a contrast with lower-growing plants. This variation concentrates entirely on low-growing conifers. This makes the design particularly suitable for use as ground cover planting or to create a foreground to some other feature in the garden that you might wish to emphasize. It could, for instance, be used in front of a house to add character to a particularly dramatic frontage or a long sweeping drive. It would also enhance a backdrop of taller specimen trees or a wall covered in climbers. Use the following plants to replace those listed in our original plan.

April

6 *Juniperus sabina* 'Tamariscifolia'

3 *Juniperus squamata* 'Blue Star'

5 *Thuja orientalis* 'Aurea Nana'

4 *Juniperus horizontalis*

2 *Pinus sylvestris* 'Beuvronensis'

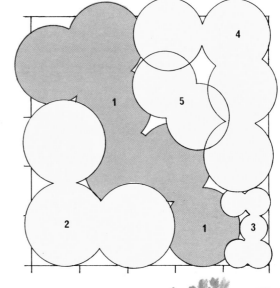

1 *Juniperus sabina* **2** *Juniperus squamata*
3 *Thuja* **4** *Juniperus horizontalis* **5** *Pinus*

JUNIPERUS SQUAMATA (short)

JUNIPERUS HORIZONTALIS (dwarf)

PINUS (short)

April Follow exactly the method of planting described on page 96.

Follow the instructions given for maintenance on pages 96 and 98.

With Ground Cover

This final variation includes evergreen ground-cover plants and a variety of foliage textures. Use the following plants:

April

6 *Erica carnea* 'Pink Spangles'

6 *Erica carnea* 'Springwood White'

1 *Abies koreana*

5 *Cotoneaster horizontalis*

5 *Genista lydia*

1 *Chamaecyparis lawsoniana* 'Ellwoodii'

1 *Chamaecyparis obtusa* 'Nana Gracilis'

From the garden shed

About 2½yd (3m) flexible wire, to cut into 8 inch (20cm) lengths

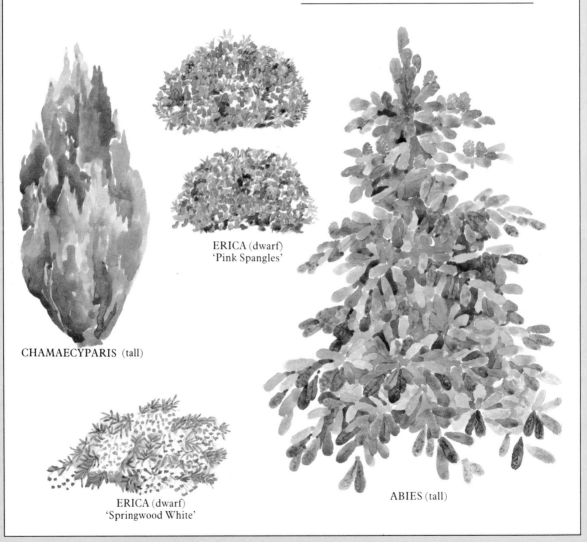

CHAMAECYPARIS (tall)

ERICA (dwarf) 'Pink Spangles'

ERICA (dwarf) 'Springwood White'

ABIES (tall)

1 *Erica* 'Pink Spangles': November–May
2 *Erica* 'Springwood White': November– May
3 *Abies*   **4** *Cotoneaster*: June (flowers);
September–December (redberries)
5 *Genista*: May–June
6 *Chamaecyparis lawsoniana*
7 *Chamaecyparis obtusa*

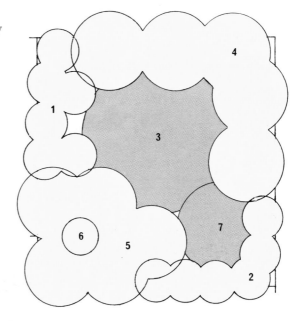

April   Prepare the ground and plant the abies and chamaecyparis as described on page 96. Plant the erica, cotoneaster and genista at the same time, following exactly the same method.

COTONEASTER (short)

GENISTA (short)

May   When the flowers of erica are over, clip the plants lightly with hedging shears to remove the dead flowers and reshape them slightly. Do not cut them back hard.

> **In subsequent years**, repeat the clipping of erica annually; this way you should never need to do any drastic reshaping of the plants, but if harder pruning is required, avoid cutting into the old wood near the base of the plants as this may kill them.
>
> Do not prune or clip genista – the plants grow into a very pleasing shape without it, and it can in fact be harmful to them.

June, July, August   Early in June, cut back late-flowering erica, as described above.

Peg down the shoots of cotoneaster with pieces of bent wire formed into 'hairpins'. This is to hold them in place as they grow, encouraging them to spread as widely as possible over the space allocated to them.

Shrub Borders

Shrubs are among the most varied and colourful plants in the garden, offering a wide range of attractions right round the year without taking much time or work to look after. They offer flowers, berries, evergreen foliage, autumn tints, coloured leaves and scented flowers, making them an ideal choice for a constantly changing focal area in the garden.

Shrubs take time to become established, so much of the maintenance is in subsequent years, rather than in the first year of planting.

Ingredients for a border 15ft × 15ft (4.5m × 4.5m)

April

3 *Mahonia aquifolium*
1 *Berberis darwinii*
3 *Azalea* 'Elizabeth'
6 *Cotoneaster horizontalis*
3 *Genista lydia*
1 *Viburnum tinus*
1 *Kerria japonica* 'Pleniflora'
5 *Spiraea × bumalda* 'Gold Flame'

From the garden shed

12 × 2 gal (10 litre) bucketfuls of bark chippings, peat, or well-rotted garden compost or manure for mulching (optional)
6lb 4oz (2.8kg) Growmore fertilizer
2 × 2 gal (10 litre) bucketfuls of moss peat

Tools required

Spade
Fork
Rake
Garden line
Hand trowel
Watering can or hose and lawn sprinkler
Secateurs
Shears
Residual weedkiller (optional)
Hoe (optional)

KERRIA (medium)

Method

Choose a site that is sunny or partly shaded for your shrub bed. It should ideally receive direct sunlight for at least half the day. The bed should be cut into a lawn, as the plan is for an island scheme which has been designed to be viewed from all round. Being a formal shape, the bed will look best if it is aligned to run parallel with any existing straight features in the garden, such as the side of the house, the garden fence or a path. However, the same design could be easily adapted to make a 'teardrop'-shaped bed, which could be tailored into a contour in the ground to suit a less formal garden.

Mark out the bed with a garden line or four canes and a ball of string. Cut out, using the spade the wrong way round so that it enters the soil at right angles to it, giving a neat edge.

Prepare the soil as described in the introduction.

Most shrubs are sold in pots, but some are 'root wrapped', that is they come with a ball of soil round their roots, wrapped in sacking.

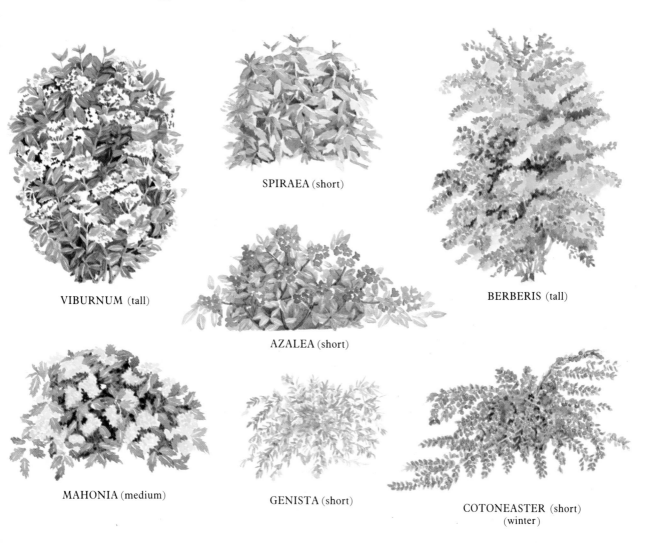

VIBURNUM (tall)

SPIRAEA (short)

BERBERIS (tall)

AZALEA (short)

MAHONIA (medium)

GENISTA (short)

COTONEASTER (short)
(winter)

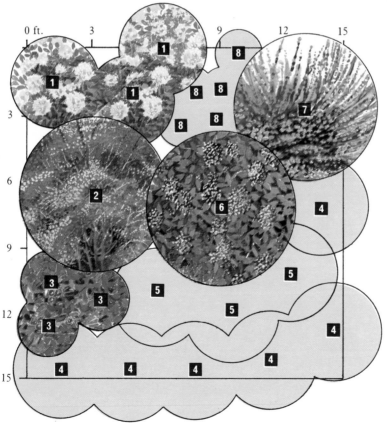

Above Shrub border. **Left** Plan for the border. Coloured areas indicate shrubs in flower in spring. Average flowering periods are listed below:

1 *Mahonia*: March–April
2 *Berberis*: April–May
3 *Azaleas*: April–May
4 *Cotoneaster*: June (flowers); September–December (red berries) **5** *Genista*: May–June **6** *Viburnum*: November–May **7** *Kerria*: April–May **8** *Spiraea*: July–August

April

Before planting   Give plants in pots a thorough watering and let them stand for 12 hours. If you are using root-wrapped plants, untie the wrappings and soak the roots in a bucket of water for an hour. Try not to remove any soil from around the roots. Then stand the shrubs in their positions on the bed next to the marker canes, turning them so that their best side faces towards the edge of the bed.

Planting   Plant pot-grown shrubs by digging a hole big enough to take the pot, leaving its rim level with the surrounding soil. Fork over the soil at the bottom of the hole to loosen it. When planting azaleas, mix in one 2 gal (10 litre) bucketful of moss peat.

Next, if the plant is in a rigid pot knock it out, giving the bottom of the pot a sharp tap with the handle of the trowel. If the pot is thin polythene, cut it away, being careful not to slice into the rootball.

Check the base of the rootball; if it is a mass of tightly coiled roots, gently tease a few of these out.

Stand the plant in the hole, facing the outside of the bed then fill in round the roots with soil. Finally, firm down round the rootball with your foot.

To plant root-wrapped shrubs, dig a hole slightly wider than the rootball and about the same depth. Fork over the bottom of the hole to loosen the soil; when planting azaleas, mix one 2 gal (10 litre) bucketful of moss peat into the soil at the bottom of the planting hole at this stage.

Without breaking the rootball up, stand the plant in the hole. Make sure it is level with the surrounding soil surface.

Water the new shrubs in, giving each one about 1 gal (4.5 litres) of water.

MAINTENANCE

Mulch the entire surface of the bed, if required, with a layer of bark chippings, peat or well-rotted garden compost or manure.

Whether you mulch the bed or not, it is essential to mulch the azaleas with peat. Apply a bucketful in a circle about 12 inches (30cm) wide round the plant. If your soil is not naturally slightly acid, use moss peat, which is acid.

The following year, feed the bed by scattering Growmore evenly over the soil at 4oz (100g) per sq yd (sq m). Hoe the fertilizer in and water thoroughly if the soil is dry.

Apply residual weedkiller to the bed to prevent weeds growing for the rest of the season. Or mulch the bed with peat or well-rotted compost or manure.

Mulch the azaleas with a bucketful of moss peat, spreading it in a circle around the plant over an area the same diameter as that covered by the branches.

In subsequent years, repeat the annual cycle of feeding, mulching, weeding or applying residual weedkiller. Always mulch the azaleas with moss peat.

No regular pruning is needed for berberis, but when the plants become large you can remove a few of the oldest branches (covered with darker coloured skin than the young shoots). Cut them right back to ground level, using secateurs.

Cotoneaster stems can be pegged down now, using pieces of wire bent over to make 'hairpins'. This encourages them to spread over the bed and they will normally take root where they are pinned, thus growing into new plants and covering the ground very effectively. Cotoneaster can be cut back if some shoots are too long.

Azalea 'Elizabeth' does not need regular pruning; just cut out any dead or broken branches.

Mahonia should not be pruned until the end of the month, by which time the flowers are over. Regular pruning is not necessary, but when the plants get big, cut a few of the oldest branches right back to ground level to encourage the production of plenty of new young shoots.

If mahonia grows badly out of shape it can, if necessary, be cut back very hard without harm.

May

Water newly planted shrubs whenever the soil is dry. Weed regularly every 1–2 weeks, if required.

> **In subsequent years**, remove the dead flower heads of the azaleas, nipping them off between thumb and forefinger. Do not use secateurs.
>
> Prune viburnum if necessary after the flowers are over. Remove dead or broken branches at their junction with a healthy shoot, and cut out a few of the oldest (darker) branches once the plants look overgrown. Cut them right out at the base of the plant.
>
> Prune kerria after the flowers are over. Cut out all the shoots that have flowered, right back to their junction with strong, healthy young shoots near the base of the plant. When the plant has grown large and the new shoots look overcrowded, thin them out slightly by cutting the thinnest shoots off at ground level.
>
> Weed or hoe regularly unless a residual weedkiller was used in spring. If weeds such as thistles, nettles or docks come up in the bed, paint them with Glyphosate gel, or dab them with a weed stick of the sort used to treat daisies in lawns.
>
> Water only in very dry spells.

June, July

Continue weeding regularly, by hand or using a hoe.

Alternatively, if you did not mulch, you could use a residual weedkiller instead. Choose one that is especially intended for use between shrubs. Remove any weeds present first then sprinkle the granules evenly over the soil, following the manufacturer's instructions. If any get on the shrub foliage wash it off with the hose, as otherwise it may scorch the leaves slightly. A single application should keep the ground free of weeds for the rest of the season.

One important point to note is *not* to remove the dead flower heads from mahonia, berberis or cotoneaster. Do not prune or cut back genista.

Continue to water the plants whenever the soil is dry.

August

Continue weeding and watering.

Late in the month, remove the dead flower heads from spiraea, using secateurs, as soon as they are over.

25ft × 15ft (7.6m × 4.5m) Border

Here the same basic plan is extended by adding some extra plants for the benefit of those with larger gardens to fill. Again, the additions have been chosen to be as representative as possible of the full range of attractions shrubs have to offer. To the list of plants given in the basic plan, you will need to add the following:

April

10 *Euonymus fortunei* 'Emerald 'n' Gold'

1 *Weigela florida* 'Foliis Purpureis'

15 *Potentilla fruticosa*

3 *Lavandula spica* 'Hidcote' (Lavender)

3 *Hebe* 'Autumn Glory'

3 *Hebe* 'Great Orme'

1 *Cornus alba* 'Elegantissima'

1 *Cytisus* × *kewensis*

1 *Cotinus coggygria*

HEBE (medium) 'Great Orme'

POTENTILLA (medium)

CORNUS (tall)

EUONYMUS (short)

WEIGELA (medium)

CYTISUS (short)

COTINUS (tall)

HEBE (short) 'Autumn Glory'

LAVANDULA (short)

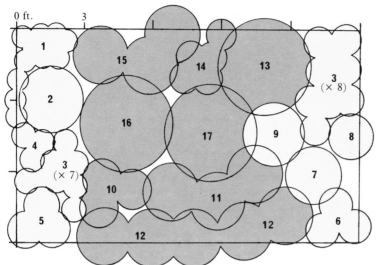

1 *Euonymus* **2** *Weigela*: May–June **3** *Potentilla*: May–August **4** *Lavender*: July–September **5** *Hebe* 'Autumn Glory': July–September **6** *Hebe* 'Great Orme': July–September **7** *Cornus* **8** *Cytisus:* May **9** *Cotinus:* July **10** *Azalea* **11** *Genista* **12** *Cotoneaster* **13** *Kerria* **14** *Spiraea* **15** *Mahonia* **16** *Berberis* **17** *Viburnum*

April Prepare the border as described on page 105, but extend its length by 10ft (3m). Following the method on page 107, plant new shrubs as in plan.

August Lightly clip potentilla with hedging shears to remove the dead flowers and reshape the plants.

September Towards the end of the month, clip lavender lightly with shears to remove the dead flower heads and reshape the plants. Never cut back into the dark-coloured wood near the base of the plants.

Remove the dead flower heads of hebe.

In subsequent years, in **March**, cut out the oldest (dark and dull) stems of cornus, taking them right back down to ground level.

Cut back long or untidy branches of cotinus to a convenient junction with another shoot. Towards the end of the month, cut back hebe slightly to reshape the plant and remove shoots damaged during the winter. *Euonymus fortunei* is unlikely to need any pruning or clipping.

In **May**, clip cytisus lightly with shears after the flowers are over to remove the tips of the flowering shoots and tidy the plant.

In **June**, cut a few old branches of weigela right down to ground level as soon as it has finished flowering each year.

In **September**, repeat the clipping of lavender annually after flowering.

Replacement and additional plants are given at the start of each variation. For quantities of 'original' plants, uncoloured in the planting plan and not given in the variation ingredients, check with the list at the start of the main plan.

Emphasizing Foliage

This variation keeps the same basic pattern as the original plan but this time changes the plants entirely, giving a shrub garden where the emphasis is on foliage. For the original plants, substitute the following:

April

13 *Euonymus fortunei* 'Emerald 'n' Gold' (replace *Mahonia aquifolium* and *Spiraea × bumalda* 'Gold Flame')

1 *Cornus alba* 'Elegantissima' (replaces *Berberis darwinii*)

4 *Mahonia aquifolium* (replace *Azalea* 'Elizabeth' and *Genista lydia*)

11 *Euonymus fortunei* 'Silver Queen' (replace *Cotoneaster horizontalis*)

1 *Cotinus coggygria* (replaces *Viburnum tinus*)

1 *Elaeagnus pungens* 'Maculata' (replaces *Kerria japonica* 'Pleniflora')

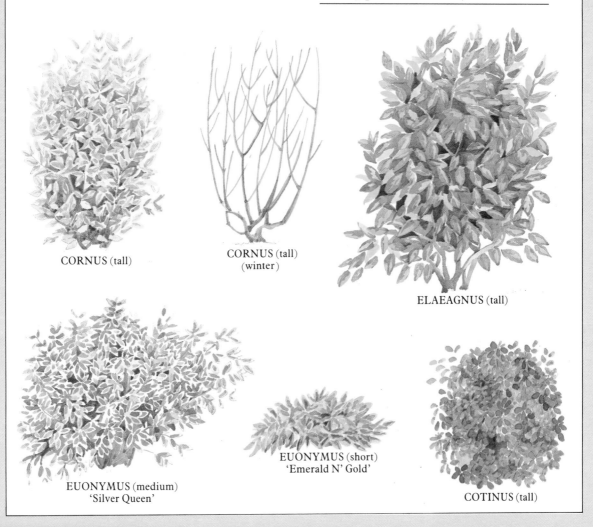

CORNUS (tall)

CORNUS (tall)
(winter)

ELAEAGNUS (tall)

EUONYMUS (medium)
'Silver Queen'

EUONYMUS (short)
'Emerald N' Gold'

COTINUS (tall)

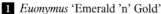

1 *Euonymus* 'Emerald 'n' Gold'
2 *Cornus*   3 *Mahonia*   4 *Cotinus*
5 *Elaeagnus*   6 *Euonymus* 'Silver Queen'

April   Follow the same method as described on pages 105 and 107 for preparing the bed, planting and establishing the plants.

In subsequent years, in **March**, cut out all the oldest stems of cornus, taking them right back down to ground level. The old shoots can easily be recognized by the fact that their bark has lost its bright red colouring and become dark and dull. These are removed to encourage new young shoots and maintain the bright red stem colour, which is particularly conspicuous in winter.

Cut back any long or untidy branches of cotinus to a convenient junction with another shoot, sufficient to tidy the plant when it becomes overgrown.

In **April**, trim the euonymus 'Silver Queen' with shears every year to maintain the height at around 1–2ft (30–61cm). This is best done now, at the start of the growing season, so that any leaves cut in half by the trimming are quickly covered by new growth.

Euonymus 'Emerald 'n' Gold' is unlikely to need any pruning or clipping.

In **June, July, August**, remove any plain green shoots from the variegated evergreen elaeagnus as soon as you notice them.

Year-Round Colour

This variation presents a complete change of plants while still keeping the same basic pattern of the main plan, this time to produce a shrub border which relies mainly on flowers for all-year-round colour. Buy the following plants to replace those shown in brackets.

April

1 *Viburnum tinus* (replaces *Berberis darwinii*)

1 *Daphne odora* (replaces *Azalea* 'Elizabeth')

4 *Genista lydia* and
1 *Hamamelis mollis* 'Pallida'
   (replace *Cotoneaster horizontalis*)

4 *Cytisus kewensis* (replace *Genista lydia*)

1 *Forsythia* × *intermedia* 'Spectabilis' (replaces *Viburnum tinus*)

1 *Philadelphus* 'Belle Etoile' (replaces *Kerria japonica* 'Pleniflora')

3 *Spiraea* × *bumalda* 'Anthony Waterer'

1 *Potentilla fruticosa*,
1 *Hypericum* 'Hidcote',
1 *Hibiscus syriacus*, and
4 *Cytisus kewensis*
   (replace *Spiraea* × *bumalda* 'Gold Flame' and *Mahonia aquifolium*)

PHILADELPHUS (tall)

DAPHNE (medium)

FORSYTHIA (tall)

POTENTILLA (medium)

HAMAMELIS (tall)

SPIRAEA (medium)

CYTISUS (short)

HIBISCUS (tall)

HYPERICUM (medium)

1 *Viburnum*   2 *Daphne*: January–April
3 *Genista*   4 *Cytisus*: May
5 *Forsythia*: March–April
6 *Philadelphus*: June–July   7 *Spiraea*
8 *Potentilla*: May–August   9 *Hibiscus*:
July–October   10 *Hamamelis*: January
11 *Hypericum*: June–September
12 *Cytisus*

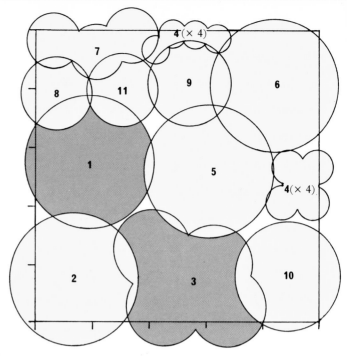

April   Follow the method described on pages 105 and 107 for preparing the bed, planting and establishing the plants.

After planting, prune back the shoots of forsythia by about half, cutting them off above a leaf joint.

In subsequent years, in **February**, cut back broken or straggly hamamelis stems, after flowering, cutting to their junction with another branch.

In **March**, prune hypericum, shortening the longest shoots to keep it in shape.

In **April**, prune forsythia after flowering. Cut any damaged or dead shoots back to healthy wood and remove a few of the oldest (darker) branches back to the junction with a main branch or ground level.

In **May**, clip cytisus with shears after flowering to remove tips of flowering shoots and tidy the plant.

In **July**, prune philadelphus after the flowers are over. Cut out some of the oldest shoots each year to their junction with another branch.

In **August**, clip potentilla with hedging shears after flowering to remove the dead heads and keep the plant a good shape.

Clip the dead flower heads from the spiraea and, after several years, start to remove a few of the oldest branches. No pruning is needed for daphne.

November   Hibiscus requires no regular pruning; just shorten long shoots immediately after flowering.

Fragrant

The final variation on the shrub theme concentrates on creating an area of garden which will be rich in fragrance. For the plants in the original plan, substitute the following:

April

---

3 *Chaenomeles speciosa*, and
7 *Lavandula spica* 'Hidcote' (lavender)
(replace *Mahonia aquifolium*)

---

1 *Philadelphus* 'Belle Etoile' (replaces *Berberis darwinii*)

---

1 *Daphne odora* 'Aureomarginata'

---

15 *Lavandula spica* 'Hidcote' (lavender)

---

1 *Hamamelis mollis* 'Pallida', and
1 *Rosa* 'Boule de Neige'
(replace *Azalea* 'Elizabeth', *Cotoneaster horizontalis* and *Genista lydia*)

---

1 *Buddleia davidii* (replaces *Viburnum tinus*)

---

1 *Viburnum fragrans* (replaces *Kerria japonica* 'Pleniflora')

---

1 *Rosmarinus officinalis* (replaces *Spiraea × bumalda* 'Gold flame')

ROSA (tall)

VIBURNUM (tall)

BUDDLEIA (tall)

LAVANDULA (short)

ROSMARINUS (tall)

CHAENOMELES (medium)

PHILADELPHUS (tall)

HAMAMELIS (tall)

DAPHNE (medium)

April Prepare and plant the bed in exactly the same way as described on page 107.

June, July Deadhead the rose regularly, cutting back to the next full size leaf down the stem.

1 *Philadelphus*: June–July **2** *Daphne*: January–April **3** *Lavender*: July–September **4** *Rose* June–October **5** *Buddleia*: July–October **6** *Viburnum* **7** *Rosemary* **8** *Chaenomeles*: January–April **9** *Hamamelis*: January

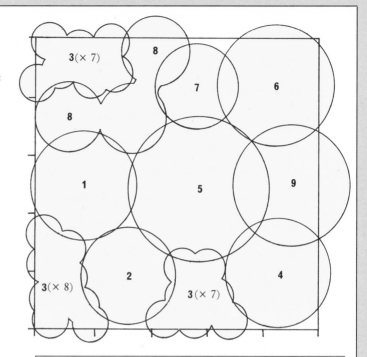

In subsequent years, in **February**, cut back broken or straggly hamamelis stems to another branch.

In **March**, cut buddleia shoots that flowered the previous year down to within 6–8 inches (15–20cm) of the dark, older wood.

Prune rose 'Boule de Neige' by cutting away weak, twiggy shoots and dead growth. No other pruning is needed.

In **April**, cut out dead, damaged or overcrowded viburnum branches after flowering. Cut out dead or browning shoots of rosemary, and shorten tall branches.

In **May**, thin out overcrowded chaenomeles branches by cutting back to another branch after flowering.

In **August**, cut some of the oldest philadelphus shoots to another branch after flowering. Daphne is not pruned.

In **September**, clip lavender with shears after flowering to remove dead flowers and reshape the plant.

In **October**, prune rose 'Boule de Neige' after flowering: cut out dead, damaged or weak shoots and shorten tips of shoots slightly to remove soft growth before winter.

Dry, Sunny Beds

How do you turn a 'problem' dry border into an easily maintained and attractive feature that will grace any garden? The secret lies in using plants that actually prefer dry living conditions, instead of struggling to grow 'ordinary' garden plants in places that don't suit them. Then, using a pleasing design, you can easily create an unusual and stylish border. The main plan here makes the most of a hot, dry area by converting it into a Mediterranean border that will act as a permanent reminder of holidays in the sun.

Ingredients for a dry, sunny border 15ft × 4ft (4.5m × 1.2m)

April

1 *Rosmarinus officinalis* 'Jessop's Upright' (rosemary)

1 *Juniperus squamata* 'Blue Star' (juniper)

3 *Perovskia atriplicifolia*

1 *Santolina chamaecyparissus*

1 *Senecio* 'Sunshine'

6 *Dianthus* 'Doris'

2 *Helianthemum nummularium* 'Wisley Pink'

8 *Iberis* 'Giant Hyacinth'

3 *Lavandula spica* 'Hidcote' (lavender)

From the garden shed

Small packet of slug pellets

30 × 2 gal (10 litre) bucketfuls of coarse rock chippings (optional)

Tools required

Spade

Fork

Rake

Garden line

Hand trowel

Watering can or hose

Shears

Secateurs

Method

Choose a sunny but reasonably well-sheltered site, and mark out a rectangle 15ft (4.5m) long by 4ft (1.2m) wide, using a garden line. Cut alongside the line with a spade to form the boundary of the bed. Use the spade the wrong way round so that the blade goes into the soil vertically, giving a nice clean edge which can easily be kept tidy. Now take away the line, and prepare the soil as described in the introduction.

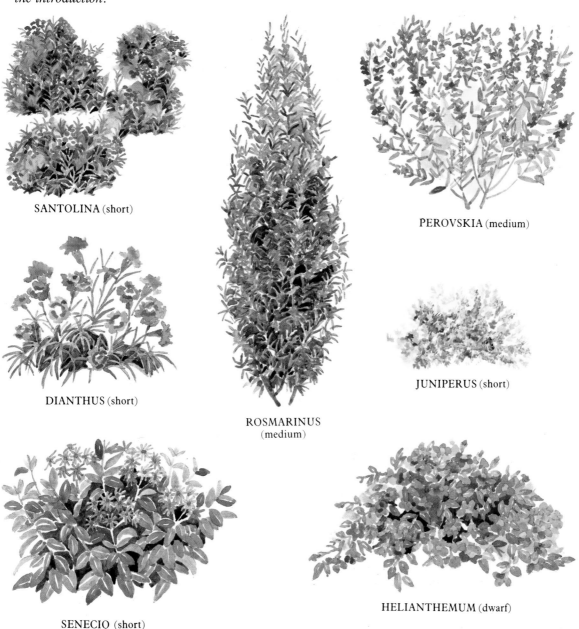

SANTOLINA (short)

PEROVSKIA (medium)

DIANTHUS (short)

JUNIPERUS (short)

ROSMARINUS (medium)

SENECIO (short)

HELIANTHEMUM (dwarf)

April

Planting To plant the rosemary, juniper, perovskia, santolina, senecio, dianthus, helianthemum and lavender, check with the plan and stand them, still in their pots, roughly in position. Turn each plant so that its 'best' side faces the front of the border.

Start planting from the back of the bed, lifting each pot in turn and marking its exact position with the trowel. Dig a small hole the same depth as the pot in the position you have marked and gently knock the plant out by tapping the base of its pot with the trowel. Taking great care not to break up the ball of roots, place the plant into its hole. The top of the rootball should now be level with the surface of the surrounding soil. If it is not, add or subtract a little soil from the bottom of the hole to level it up. Double check that the best side of the plant is still facing the front and fill in round the roots with soil. Finish off by firming the soil down lightly round the plant using the handle of the trowel.

MAINTENANCE

The day after planting, check the iberis to see if they need watering again.

Once a week, check all the plants in the bed and water them if the soil is very dry.

(April)

To plant the iberis just peel the container away if it is the flexible sort or, if it is rigid, loosen the plants by tapping the tray down on a hard surface once or twice. You can then simply tip them out. Separate each plant from the solid mass of roots by tearing them carefully apart, leaving them with a roughly equal-sized ball of roots. Lay them out in position and, as you come to plant, lift each in turn and mark its position with a trowel. Dig a hole about 1 inch (2.5cm) deeper than each rootball and plant so that the tops of the roots are slightly below the surface of the soil.

When you have laid out the whole bed, water each plant in with a watering can or hose. Give the rosemary, juniper, lavender, perovskia, santolina and senecio approximately ½ gal (2 litres) of water each, and the iberis, helianthemum and dianthus about 1pt (500ml) each.

To finish the bed off, apply a layer of rock chippings all over the surface of the bed as a 'top-dressing', at the rate of two bucketfuls of chippings per yard run of bed. This is not essential and can be left out if you prefer, but it looks very ornamental and is very beneficial too, helping to smother out germinating weed seedlings and retain moisture in the soil.

Sprinkle a few slug pellets between the iberis plants.

Opposite Dry, sunny bed. **Below** Plan for the bed. Coloured areas indicate plants in flower in midsummer. Average flowering periods are listed below: **1** *Rosemary* **2** *Juniper* **3** *Perovskia*: August–September **4** *Santolina*: July **5** *Senecio*: June–July **6** *Dianthus*: June–July, September–October **7** *Helianthemum*: June–July **8** *Iberis*: July–September **9** *Lavender*: July–September

(April)

In subsequent years, cut back any shoots of rosemary that have been 'burnt' by cold weather or wind during the winter. Cut back a whole shoot at a time right to the point where it originates from a main branch.

If santolina or senecio become overgrown, this is the time to cut back the untidy shoots to their base.

Lavender can also be pruned lightly now, but avoid cutting back into the dark old wood from which it is difficult for new shoots to regenerate. Cut broken or awkwardly shaped juniper branches back to a main branch or the stem.

Use secateurs for all these jobs. Give the entire bed its annual feed. Scatter 2oz (50g) of Growmore per sq yd (sq m) evenly over the soil surface and hoe it lightly in.

Plant new iberis as before and water them in.

Follow up by applying more rock chippings if the previous layer is looking in need of a top-up. You will need very much less material now than you used in the first place and 7–8 bucketfuls should be sufficient.

May

Continue to check all the plants and water if the soil is dry.

July

Using secateurs, cut the faded flower heads from dianthus late in the month. They will then sometimes go on to produce a second flush of flowers later. Cut back the helianthemum after flowering to remove the tips of the shoots complete with dead flowers, and to encourage a second flowering between August and November. Water the juniper in dry weather to prevent foliage from browning.

September

Pull out the iberis plants when they are over. Use shears to clip off the dead flower heads from lavender and santolina and lightly trim the plants into compact, bushy shapes.

Use secateurs to remove the dead flower heads from perovskia and senecio. This is just to tidy the bushes; do not actually prune them now.

Rosemary, being slow growing, will not need pruning, but cut out entirely, with the secateurs, any shoots that have become broken, or which are starting to spoil the shape of the plant by growing out at odd angles.

If dianthus and helianthemum produced a second flush of flowers, remove the dead heads, as above, as soon as the petals start to fade.

Dry and Shady

This variation is for a different type of dry site – this time a shady one. Again, by using plants that suit the conditions, you will have no trouble in growing an attractive border and in fact the one here, by including evergreens and spring bulbs, looks good all year round. By way of a bonus, it also requires very little maintenance. Buy the plants listed here in place of those shown in brackets.

March

1 *Berberis thunbergii* 'Atropurpurea' (replaces *Perovskia atriplicifolia* and *Santolina chamaecyparissus*)

1 *Sambucus canadensis* 'Aurea' (replaces *Senecio* 'Sunshine')

3 *Polygonum affine* 'Donald Lowndes' (replace *Dianthus* 'Doris')

3 *Salvia officinalis* 'Purpurea' (replace *Iberis* 'Giant Hyacinth' and 1 *Helianthemum nummularium* 'Wisley Pink')

1 *Bergenia* 'Ballawley Hybrids' (replaces 1 *Helianthemum nummularium* 'Wisley Pink')

1 *Alchemilla mollis* (replaces 1 *Lavandula spica* 'Hidcote')

1 *Cotoneaster conspicuus* 'Decorus' (replaces 2 *Lavandula spica* 'Hidcote')

April

1 *Elaeagnus pungens* 'Maculata' (replaces *Rosmarinus officinalis* 'Jessop's Upright')

5 *Ajuga reptans* (replace *Juniperus squamata* 'Blue Star')

September

30 *Anemone blanda* (replace *Juniperus squamata* 'Blue Star')

From the garden shed

Substitute bark chippings for stone, for an authentic shade-garden finish

POLYGONUM (dwarf)

AJUGA (dwarf)

SAMBUCUS (tall)

ALCHEMILLA (short)

BERBERIS (medium)

ELAEAGNUS (tall)

SALVIA
(short)

BERGENIA (short)

COTONEASTER
(tall)

ANEMONE
(dwarf)

March   Plant out the berberis, cotoneaster, sambucus, polygonum, salvia, bergenia and alchemilla following instructions on page 120.

April   Plant out the elaeagnus and ajuga following the instructions for rosemary etc on page 120.

> Replacement and additional plants are given at the start of each variation. For quantities of 'original' plants, uncoloured in the planting plan and not given in the variation ingredients, check with the list at the start of the main plan.

September   Plant the anemone corms. Dig holes 3 inches (7cm) deep evenly spaced among the ajuga. Drop a corm into each hole and fill with soil.

> **In subsequent years**, in **March**, deadhead anemones and cut dead foliage to ground level.
>   In **April**, shorten long straggling shoots on the elaeagnus, using secateurs. Cut damaged or dead sambucus shoots back to a healthy shoot. Shorten overlong cotoneaster branches. Cut back tips of berberis shoots that don't produce new buds when the rest of the plant does.

June   Keep the bed free of weeds. Snip off the dead flower heads from bergenia.

July   Remove dead heads from ajuga by clipping lightly over the plant with shears.
   Cut back dead flower stems and old foliage only of alchemilla. Late in the month cut down and remove dead flower stems and foliage from the polygonum.

November   Cut the salvia down to ground level.

1 *Elaeagnus*   **2** *Ajuga*: June–July   **3** *Anemones*: February–April   **4** *Berberis*: March–May   **5** *Sambucus*: July   **6** *Polygonum*: June   **7** *Salvia*: June–July   **8** *Bergenia*: April–May   **9** *Alchemilla*: June–August   **10** *Cotoneaster*: October–December (berries)

Exposed

Yet another 'difficult' site. Here it is planted with a scheme designed to cope with the worst of wind and weather yet still look attractive. Substitute the plants shown here for those in brackets from the original dry border plan.

March

1 *Spiraea × bumalda* 'Anthony Waterer' (replaces *Rosmarinus officinalis* 'Jessop's Upright')

4 *Scabiosa caucasica* 'Clive Greaves' (scabious), and
3 *Polygonum affine* 'Donald Lowndes' (replace *Perovskia atriplicifolia*, *Santolina chamaecyparissus* and *Dianthus* 'Doris')

1 *Berberis thunbergii* 'Atropurpurea' (replaces *Lavandula spica* 'Hidcote')

From the garden shed

30 × 2 gal (10 litre) bucketfuls of stone chippings, peat or well-rotted manure or garden compost

7½oz (212g) sulphate of potash

April

1 *Euonymus fortunei* 'Silver Queen' (replaces *Senecio* 'Sunshine')

6 *Saxifraga moschata* 'Cloth of Gold' (saxifrage) (replace *Helianthemum nummularium* 'Wisley Pink' and *Iberis* 'Giant Hyacinth')

EUONYMUS (medium)

SAXIFRAGA (dwarf)

POLYGONUM (dwarf)

BERBERIS (medium)

SCABIOUS (short)

SPIRAEA (medium)

March   Plant out the spiraea, scabious, polygonum and berberis following the instructions for rosemary etc on page 120.

April   Plant out the euonymus and saxifrage following the instructions for rosemary etc on page 120.

After planting, top dress with stone chippings or organic material such as peat, well-rotted old manure or garden compost. Water the soil thoroughly before applying the top dressing.

In subsequent years, reapply the top dressing to the surface of the bed as the plants are starting back into growth (7–8 bucketfuls of material). At the same time you will be able to see if there is any 'die-back' on the spiraea and berberis – tips of shoots that do not produce new buds when the rest of the plant does, showing that they have been killed by cold weather. Cut these tips back with secateurs to a point where new buds can be seen growing strongly.

August   Apply 1½oz (15g) sulphate of potash per sq yd (sq m) of the soil in the bed. Water it in well. This may help to encourage the new growth to ripen, hardening it ready to withstand the bad weather to come.

September   Cut back and remove the dead flower stems and foliage from scabious and polygonum as soon as they start to die back naturally, using secateurs.

November   Cut saxifrage and scabious stems down to ground level using secateurs.

Prune any dead or badly browned branches of the euonymus with secateurs right back to a main branch.

1 *Spiraea*: July–August   **2** *Scabious*: June–September
3 *Polygonum*: June   **4** *Euonymus*
5 *Saxifrage*: April–May   **6** *Berberis*: March–May
7 *Juniper*

Island Bed

For something completely different, you can depart from the traditional idea of plants growing round the edges of the garden next to a hedge or fence, and instead opt for a modern alternative – an island bed. Here the plants are in the middle, with the lawn round the edge – perfect for a front garden, or in a small town garden surrounded by paving instead of grass. The great advantage of an island bed is that it not only looks striking but is easy to maintain, since you can reach all parts without having to walk on the soil. This variation uses most of the same plants as the main dry border plan, re-arranged to create an entirely different effect. You will need to buy the following additional plants:

March

6 *Ajuga reptans* (extra)

4 *Polygonum affine* 'Donald Lowndes' (extra)

April

1 *Yucca filamentosa* (replaces *Senecio* 'Sunshine')

1 *Juniperus horizontalis* 'Banff' (juniper) (replaces *Juniperus squamata* 'Blue Star')

From the garden shed

27 × 2 gal (10 litre) bucketfuls of stone or bark chippings (optional)

YUCCA (short)

POLYGONUM (dwarf)

AJUGA (dwarf)

JUNIPERUS (dwarf)

Mark out the bed, a circle with a diameter of 9ft (2.75m), following the instructions on page 119. For a less formal bed, elongate the shape slightly to form a 'teardrop', tailored to fit into a contour in the ground for a really 'designed' look. Prepare the soil as described on page 113.

1 *Yucca* **2** *Juniper* **3** *Ajuga*: June–July
4 *Polygonum*: June **5** *Lavender*
6 *Santolina* **7** *Helianthemum*
8 *Dianthus* **9** *Iberis*
10 *Perovskia* **11** *Rosemary*

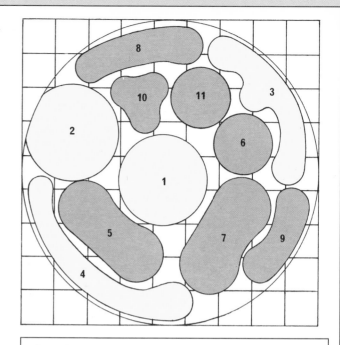

March   Plant out ajuga and polygonum following instructions for rosemary etc on page 120.

April   Plant out the juniper following the instructions for rosemary etc on page 120. If winters are severe in your area – leave the yucca in its pot and plant that too. Dig a hole the same size as the pot, and sink it up to its rim in the ground. After planting and watering spread bark or stone chippings in a thin layer all over the bed.

In subsequent years, if the yucca is damaged by frost, prune it back hard with secateurs until you are cutting into live healthy tissue (which will appear creamy green in colour as against the brown of dead tissue). Cut broken or awkwardly shaped juniper branches back to a main branch or stem.

July   Clip lightly over ajuga with shears to remove dead flower heads.

September   Use secateurs to cut back and remove the dead flower stems and foliage from the polygonum.

October   Dig the yucca out, still in its pot, and put it in a frost-free greenhouse or porch until March or April. If you planted your yucca in the ground, give it protection in very frosty or windy weather by gathering up its leaves and wrapping them round like a 'haycock' with newspaper or old fabric held in place with string. This can only be done for a week or two at a time, or the leaves may turn yellow or drop off.

With Annuals

The final variation adds colourful annual flowers to the basic plan to bring a touch of seasonal variation to the dry border. In subsequent years you may like to add ideas of your own – it is easy to experiment with annuals, using them to provide a very different look.

May

Buy the following additional plants:

8 *Osteospermum* 'Polestar' (replace *Santolina chamaecyparissus* and 1 of 3 *Perovskia atriplicifolia*)

7 *Tagetes patula* 'Suzy Wong' (French marigold) (replace *Dianthus* 'Doris' and 1 of 2 *Helianthemum nummularium* 'Wisley Pink')

8 *Mesembryanthemum criniflorum* 'Mixed' (replace 1 of the 3 *Lavandula spica* and 1 *Helianthemum nummularium* 'Wisley Pink')

From the garden shed

6 × 2 gal (10 litre) bucketfuls of peat

MESEMBRYANTHEMUM (dwarf)

TAGETES (dwarf)

OSTEOSPERMUM
(short)

1 *Osteospermum*: July–September   **2** *Tagetes*: June–September   **3** *Mesembryanthemum*: June–September   **4** *Rosemary*   **5** *Juniper*   **6** *Perovskia*   **7** *Iberis*   **8** *Lavender*   **9** *Senecio*

Method

Prepare and plant the bed in exactly the same way as described in the basic plan on page 119. After raking the soil and marking it out, spread 2 bucketfuls of peat per sq yd (sq m) over the areas where the osteospermum, tagetes and mesembryanthemum are to be planted, and fork it lightly into the top 3–4 inches (7.5–10cm) of soil. This is to provide a moisture reserve to help them get established, as they are very shallow rooted.

May   Plant out the osteospermum, tagetes and mesembryanthemum following the instructions for iberis on page 121. Make quite sure that the mesembryanthemums are planted so that they receive the maximum sun possible, without being shaded by other plants, as their flowers only open when the sun is on them. Water each plant in with about 1pt (500ml) water.

June, July   Water all the plants whenever the soil round them is dry for the first 8 weeks to help them get established. From mid to late June onwards, use the secateurs to snip the dead flower heads from tagetes and osteospermum as soon as they are over. This will encourage them to continue producing new flowers right up to the end of the summer. Do not bother to deadhead mesembryanthemum; the individual flowers only last 1–2 days each and the plants continue flowering prolifically regardless.

September   When the tagetes, osteospermum and mesembryanthemum have stopped producing any new flowers pull them out and throw them away.

Summer Borders

Want a colourful border in an instant? This summer bedding scheme, suitable for a sunny bed backed by a hedge, fence or wall, will give you just that. By planting annuals in summer when they are already coming into flower, you can be sure of a flower-packed bed in a matter of days. Perfect if you have just moved to a new house, or have a special occasion like a family wedding when you want to make the garden look especially colourful. Ideal, too, for people who just like to ring the changes, and try something new every year!

Ingredients for a sunny border 10ft × 3ft (3m × 1m)

March

Packet *Reseda odorata* (mignonette) seeds

Packet *Nigella damascena* 'Miss Jekyll Blue' seeds

May

8 *Nicotiana alata* 'Sensation Mixed'

2 *Amaranthus caudatus*

15 *Lobelia erinus* 'Mrs Clibran'

8 *Pelargonium* 'Rose Diamond'

8 *Malcolmia maritima* (Virginian stock)

8 *Petunias* 'Resisto Mixed'

From the garden shed

Small packet of slug pellets

40oz (1kg) Growmore fertilizer

Small bottle of liquid foliar plant feed (optional)

Small tub of soil pests killer

Tools required

Spade

Fork

Rake

Garden line

Hand trowel

Watering can or hose

Secateurs or sharp scissors

Edging shears (if bed is surrounded by grass)

Method

Mark out an oblong bed 10ft × 3ft (3m × 1m) with the garden line. Cut alongside the line with the spade to form the boundary of the border. Use the spade the wrong way round so the blade goes into the soil vertically – this gives you a nice clean edge to the grass in front of the bed, which can easily be kept tidy with edging shears later. Remove the line, and prepare the soil as described in the introduction.

NIGELLA (short)

RESEDA (short)

LOBELIA (dwarf)

MALCOLMIA (dwarf)

NICOTIANA (short)

PETUNIA (dwarf)

PELARGONIUM (short)

AMARANTHUS (medium)

March

Planting Sow the mignonette and nigella seeds. First rake the soil in the areas indicated in the plan to a fine tilth, and make sure it is level.

Then scatter the seeds where they are to flower and rake gently.

MAINTENANCE

April

Thin out the mignonette and nigella seedlings to six of each: when the first pair of leaves is fully expanded, remove excess seedlings with the tips of your thumb and index finger, leaving a space of 9 inches (23cm) around each remaining seedling.

May

Plant out the lobelia, nicotiana, amaranthus, pelargoniums, Virginian stock and petunias. Stand the pelargoniums and amaranthus in position still in their pots, allowing about 10–12 sq inches (64–77 sq cm) for the pelargoniums and 9 sq inches (58 sq cm) for the amaranthus.

The day after planting, check to see if the surface of the soil has dried out, and if so water the plants again. Continue watering like this for the first two or three weeks, until you start to see the plants growing. This indicates that they are becoming established.

0 ft.   2   4   6   8   10

(May)

Take the remaining plants out of their 'strips'. Tear away flimsy trays but remove the rigid ones by giving the base a couple of sharp taps on a concrete path then tipping the contents out. Separate the plants by gently tearing the compost apart so that each of them is left with a similarly-sized rootball. Lay them in position, allowing each a space of 9 sq inches (58 sq cm). Lift each plant and mark its position with a trowel. Plant from the back of the bed to the front.

To plant the pelargoniums and amaranthus, knock them out of their pots by tapping the base with a trowel. Dig a hole the same depth as the pot, in position, then place the plant into its hole. Check the top of the rootball is level with the top of the hole. Using a trowel, fill in with soil and firm in with the trowel handle.

To plant the nicotiana, lobelia, Virginian stock and petunias, dig a hole wide enough to take the rootball and 1 inch (2.5 cm) deeper. Put the plant into the hole, with the rootball about 1 inch (2.5cm) below the surface. Fill in with soil and lightly firm down with the trowel handle.

When you have planted the whole bed, water each plant in with approximately 1pt (500ml) of water using a watering can or hose. Sprinkle a scattering of slug pellets between plants.

Left Summer border   **Above** Planting plan. Coloured areas indicate plants in flower in midsummer. Average flowering periods are listed below.   **1** *Nicotiana*: June–September   **2** *Amaranthus*: July–September   **3** *Mignonette*: June–September   **4** *Nigella*: June–August   **5** *Lobelia*: May–September   **6** *Pelargonium*: May–September   **7** *Malcolmia*: April–August   **8** *Petunias*: June–September

---

Special note

When your garden is newly planted, you must make sure that your plants receive sufficient watering. This is particulariy important in the case of bedding plants which, being shallow-rooted, are very vulnerable to the top layer of soil drying out. After about a month, when the roots have penetrated deeper into the soil, looking at the surface of the soil is no longer enough. Stick your finger or the probe of an electronic water meter into the soil to a depth of 3–4 inches (7.5–10cm). If you are still unsure, dig out a handful of soil to the depth of the trowel and inspect it for moisture.

June

Water every few days in dry weather and about once a week if there is some natural rainfall.

An occasional foliar feed works wonders to 'boost' a good display of flowers. Choose a cool day, or wait till late evening to apply the feed. Plants must have previously been watered so that they are not under stress when you feed them, nor should the sun be on them. Dilute the feed according to the manufacturer's instructions and apply it through a fine rose on a watering can, 'watering' it on all over the plants.

Every 2–3 weeks, apply a new scattering of slug pellets.

Go over the bed once a week snipping off the dead flower heads with secateurs, to encourage new blooms. Cut as closely as possible beneath the head. Remove the dead flower heads from the bed, or they may encourage slugs or become a source of disease.

Hand weed the bed every two weeks to keep it tidy and weed-free, using a trowel. If you prefer to use a hoe, be very careful as annuals have very soft stems and are easily cut into or broken right off by careless hoeing. If the bed is set in a lawn trim the grass round the edge regularly. Each time you mow the grass, cut neatly round the edge of the border with edging shears to give a clean finish.

July

Continue watering, feeding, weeding and deadheading, as above. Apply slug pellets as long as the weather continues rainy.

August, September

Continue weeding, watering, feeding and deadheading regularly until the plants stop producing new flowers. This will probably be towards the end of September, though it can be later given a good summer.

Once the last flowers are over the plants are finished. Pull them out, remove any weeds from the bed and fork it over to leave it tidy for winter.

Colour Contrasts

If you like sharp contrasts and strong colours, this border has been created specially for you. Gone are the subtle blends of mixed varieties, and in their place are bright, hot colours grouped to create maximum impact. For this design, you will need the following additional plants which replace those shown in brackets.

May

8 *Tagetes erecta* 'Gold Galore' (African marigold) (replace *Nicotiana alata* 'Sensation Mixed')

1 *Amaranthus caudatus* 'Viridis' (replaces one of the two *Amaranthus caudatus*)

8 *Pelargonium* 'Scarlet Diamond' (replace *Pelargonium* 'Rose Diamond')

4 *Rudbeckia hirta* 'Rustic Dwarfs' (replace *Reseda odorata*)

6 *Tagetes* 'Naughty Maria' (replace *Malcolmia maritima*)

8 *Petunia* 'White Magic' (replace *Petunia* 'Resisto Mixed')

RUDBECKIA (short)

AMARANTHUS (medium)

TAGETES ERECTA (dwarf)

PELARGONIUM (short)

PETUNIA (dwarf)

TAGETES PATULA (dwarf)

May Plant the tagetes, amaranthus, pelargonium, rudbeckia and petunias following the instructions for pelargoniums etc on page 135.

> Replacement and additional plants are given at the start of each variation. For quantities of 'original' plants, uncoloured in the planting plan and not given in the variation ingredients, check with the list at the start of the main plan.

June, July Go over the bed once a week snipping off the dead flower heads to encourage new blooms; cut just below the flower heads. Hand weed the bed every two weeks, using a trowel, and trim the grass round the edge of the bed with shears, if it is set in a lawn.

August, September When the last flowers are over pull the plants out and throw them away. Fork over the bed and leave it tidy for winter.

1 *Tagetes* 'Gold Galore': June–September **2** *Amaranthus viridis*: June–September **3** *Nigella* **4** *Amaranthus caudatus* **5** *Lobelia* **6** *Pelargonium*: May– October **7** *Petunias*: June– September **8** *Rudbeckia*: July– August **9** *Tagetes* 'Naughty Maria'

VARIATION TWO

Colour Harmony

This variation comes at the opposite end of the spectrum to the previous one as far as mood is concerned. Instead of using strong colours to make lively contrasts, it employs gentle harmonies of colour to create a border that is quiet and relaxing in character. Buy the following plants to replace those shown in brackets.

March

Packet *Godetia* seeds (replace *Lobelia erinus* 'Mrs Clibran')

May

8 *Nicotiana alata* 'Lime Green' (replace *Nicotiana alata* 'Sensation Mixed')

1 *Amaranthus caudatus* 'Viridis' (replaces one of the two *Amaranthus caudatus*)

2 *Cosmos bipinnatus* 'Sensation mixed' (replace *Reseda odorata*)

6 *Gypsophila elegans* (replace *Nigella damascena* 'Miss Jekyll Blue')

8 *Petunia* Super Cascade Lilac (replace *Petunia* 'Resisto Mixed')

NICOTIANA (short)

COSMOS (medium)

GYPSOPHILA (short)

GODETIA (short)

PETUNIA (dwarf)

AMARANTHUS (medium)

March Sow godetia seeds following instructions for mignonette and nigella on page 134, covering the seeds with a maximum $\frac{1}{4}$ inch (0.5cm) of fine soil.

April Thin out the godetia seedlings to 6 inches (15cm) apart, following the instructions for mignonette and nigella on page 134.

May Plant the nicotiana, amaranthus, cosmos, gypsophila and petunias following the instructions for pelargoniums etc on page 135.

June, July Go over the bed once a week with secateurs, cutting off the dead flowers just below the heads, to encourage new blooms. Weed the bed every two weeks, and trim the grass round the edge of the bed with shears if it is set in a lawn.

August, September When the flowers are finished pull out the plants and throw them away. Remove any weeds and fork the bed over to leave it tidy for winter.

1 *Nicotiana*: June–September
2 *Amaranthus caudatus*
3 *Cosmos*: August–September
4 *Gypsophila*: May–September
5 *Amaranthus viridis*: June–September **6** *Godetia*: June–August **7** *Pelargonium*
8 *Malcolmia* **9** *Petunias*: June–September

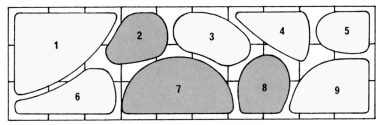

Foliage

This border is based largely on foliage effects, and is ideal for a summer when flowering plants are slow to come into bloom. You will need the following additional plants. This variation does not require the Virginian stock.

1 *Ricinus communis* 'Impala' (replaces *Nicotiana alata* 'Sensation Mixed')

1 *Humulus japonicus* 'Variegatus'

1 *Kochia trichophylla* (burning bush) (replaces one of the two *Amaranthus caudatus*)

8 *Pelargonium* 'Scarlet Diamond' (replace *Pelargonium* 'Rose Diamond')

6 *Tropaeolum majus* Climbing Mixed (nasturtium) (replace *Nigella damascena* 'Miss Jekyll Blue')

5 *Coleus blumei* (replace *Petunia* 'Resisto Mixed')

12 *Lobelia erinus* 'Mrs Clibran' (replace 15)

From the garden shed

Length of plastic-covered netting or wooden trellis measuring 6ft × 4ft (2m × 1.2m)

6 pea sticks 3ft (1m) high

3 × 5ft (1.5m) poles (if the border is backed by a hedge)

Packet of plant ties

Masonry nails or wire ties

HUMULUS
(medium)

KOCHIA (short)

TROPAEOLUM
(medium)

COLEUS (short)

PELARGONIUM (short)

Method

Before marking the bed out, secure the netting or trellis in place at the back of the border where the climbing plants (nasturtium and humulus) are to grow. If the border backs on to a wall or fence it can be fixed to this using masonry nails or wire ties. If there is a hedge behind the border, hammer the three poles in position at the back of the border and secure the netting or trellis to those.

1 *Ricinus* **2** *Humulus*
3 *Nasturtium*: June–September
4 *Kochia* **5** *Lobelia*
6 *Pelargonium*: May–October
7 *Reseda* **8** *Coleus*
9 *Amaranthus*

May To plant ricinus, burning bush, pelargonium, coleus and lobelia, follow the method described for the lobelia etc on page 134, but notice that the positions of some of the plants used in that plan have now changed. The mignonette has moved to the position previously occupied by the Virginian stock, and their original place is now occupied by nasturtium. Amaranthus has moved to the corner of the area occupied by the lobelia.

Plant the humulus and three of the nasturtiums close to their supports at the back of the border. The remaining three nasturtiums should be spaced out over the rest of their area.

RICINUS
(medium)

June Push the pea sticks in between the humulus and nasturtiums, and as the plants start to grow encourage them to ramble up and over the sticks. If necessary hold them in place with plant ties.

July, August Add a new tie to the nasturtiums and humulus every two weeks to ensure the new growth is always held firmly in place. Do the same with the nasturtiums and humulus growing against the wall, tying them regularly up to the netting or trellis to 'train' them in place.

September When the plants are starting to look past their best, at the end of the month, pull them all out and – unless you plan to repeat the same border next year – take down the supports for the climbers.

With Perennials

This variation uses old-fashioned annuals offset by perennials chosen to provide a background of silvery or creamy foliage and white flowers to create a charming cottage border. Substitute the following perennials and annuals for the plants shown in brackets.

March

1 *Gypsophila paniculata*, and
1 *Phlox paniculata* 'White Admiral'
   (replace the two *Amaranthus caudatus*)

5 *Hosta fortunei* 'Albopicta' (replace *Lobelia erinus* 'Mrs Clibran')

3 *Stachys lanata* (replace *Malcolmia maritima*)

May

10 *Lathyrus odoratus* 'Knee Hi' (sweet peas) (replace *Reseda odorata*)

From the garden shed

10 twiggy pea sticks 4ft (1.2m) high

GYPSOPHILA
(medium)

HOSTA (short)

STACHYS (dwarf)

LATHYRUS (tall)

PHLOX (short)

March Plant out the gypsophila, phlox, hosta and stachys using the method described for pelargoniums on page 135.

May Plant out the sweet peas using the method described for nicotiana etc on page 134. Push the pea sticks in between the plants. There is no need to use ties as they will scramble up the sticks by putting out tendrils.

June Check that the sweet peas are growing up the sticks and are not entangling neighbouring plants or running along the ground.

July Deadhead the sweet peas, using secateurs, as soon as the flowers are over or they will quickly stop producing new buds.

September Pull out the sweet peas as they begin to die.

November Cut back the flowers, stems and foliage of the gypsophila, phlox, hosta and stachys when they die back, using secateurs. Weed the bed and leave it tidy for winter.

1 *Nicotiana*
2 *Gypsophila*: June–August
3 *Sweet peas*: June–September
4 *Nigella*
5 *Phlox*: July–September
6 *Hosta*: July–August
7 *Pelargonium*
8 *Stachys*: July
9 *Petunias*

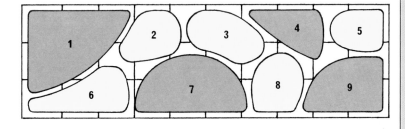

Water Gardens

Ponds are enormously adaptable, varying in character from the very formal to the totally informal, so there is one to suit every kind of garden. This chapter provides a selection of the different basic styles of water garden. The main plan is for a traditional semi-formal pond that contains something of interest for most of the year. Choose plants that are green and healthy-looking without any brown marks or rotting leaves, and where possible buy from a reputable water garden centre or specialist department in a normal garden centre.

Ingredients for a pond 8ft × 6ft (2.4m × 1.8m), with paving round the edges

April

1 *Nymphaea* 'James Brydon' (waterlily)

3 *Iris laevigata* (iris)

3 *Typha minima*

5 *Acorus gramineus* 'Variegatus'

5 *Scirpus tabernaemontani* 'Zebrinus'

3 *Hottonia palustris*

Elodea crispa (optional)

Ceratophyllum demersum (optional)

May

6 *Eichhornia crassipes*

1 *Azolla filiculoides*

Fish (optional)

From the garden shed

1 × 8ft × 6ft (2.4m × 1.8m) pre-formed plastic pond liner

$\frac{1}{2}$ cu yd (.3 cu m) of building sand

Paving slabs and cement for surrounds

Tools required

Spade

Fork

Rake

Hose

Trowel

Piece of timber

Spirit level

Method

Choose a sunny location for the pond, well away from overhanging trees.

Buy a pond liner that is graduated in three steps so as to provide different depths of water when the pond is filled. The most useful graduations would provide water 24 inches (61cm), 12 inches (30cm) and 6 inches (15cm) deep.

Construct the pond by digging out a hole several inches bigger all round than the pre-formed pond shape you have bought. Use a spade to form the rough shape and size of the pond and finish off with a trowel to give a smooth, even finish. Make sure there are no stones sticking out of the soil.

Spread a 2 inch (5cm) layer of sieved building sand evenly over the surface of the shape you have dug out. This is to provide a soft, cushioned layer to support the pond liner when it is full of water without the risk of sharp stones eventually penetrating it and making the pond leak.

Check to see how good a fit your liner is in the hole. To do this, first rake the sand lightly to leave the surface slightly indented by the points of the teeth. Now fit the liner into the hole and run a little water into it. Then bale it out, remove the liner and look at the sand to see which areas have been compressed by the weight of the water and which have not. You will be able to see easily where you need to add extra sand or remove some to achieve a perfect fit.

You will probably have to adjust the pond several times until you get a tight fit between the liner and the sand, but it is very well worth doing so. A good fit makes certain the liner is properly

CERATOPHYLLUM (dwarf)

SCIRPUS (short)

EICHHORNIA (dwarf)

TYPHA (short)

HOTTONIA (dwarf)

NYMPHAEA (short)

ACORUS (short)

IRIS (short)

AZOLLA (dwarf)

supported all round, with no areas where the plastic is stressed by the weight it is carrying. This alone will considerably extend its life.

At the same time, check repeatedly to see that the liner is lying level in the ground. This is very important too, because if it is not the water will all run to one end! To ensure it is level, lay a piece of timber lengthwise across the liner and put a spirit level on it. Move the timber and spirit level through 90 degrees and see that the liner is level crosswise too. Make any adjustments that are necessary by adding or removing sand under the liner.

When the pool is properly fitted, lay the paving round the edge and cement it in place. This can be formal paving slabs or pieces of irregularly-shaped crazy paving. You can either lay a single row of slabs round the pond or, if you prefer, continue it out to form a path or formal rectangular border round the pond. The purpose of making a border to the pond is partly to set the pond off nicely, and partly to conceal the edge of the liner which protrudes slightly above the level of the water. To make sure of hiding it lay the paving so that the edges overhang the sides of the pond slightly.

A week or two before you want to start planting, fill the pond with water so that it has a chance to warm up a little first.

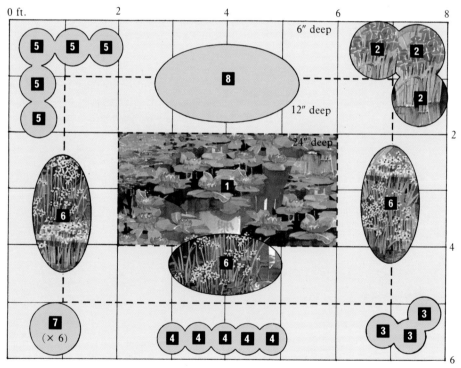

Opposite Pond. **Above** Plan for the pond. Coloured areas indicate plants in flower in early summer. Average flowering periods are listed below: **1** *Nymphaea*: June–September **2** *Iris*: June–July **3** *Typha*: September–October **4** *Acorus* **5** *Scirpus* **6** *Hottonia*: May–June **7** *Eichhornia* **8** *Azolla*

April

Planting Water plants growing in containers need only to be lowered into position. Put them in as soon as you get home to avoid any risk of them drying out or 'cooking' in polythene bags left in the sun.

Square black plastic baskets are the usual containers for water plants. Check first to see that the containers are weighted and will stay where you put them. If they are not, place a handful or two of washed horticultural gravel on top of the compost in the container.

Plants that are bought in small pots need repotting into the proper square basket containers. Choose black baskets if possible as they will not be seen from above the pond when they are submerged.

Fill the basket with John Innes seed compost and knock the water plant out of its old pot by giving the base a sharp tap with the trowel. Make a hole in the compost the same size as the rootball and plant it into this, firming lightly down round the roots.

MAINTENANCE

Do not worry if the water in your pond turns green shortly after planting. It should clear itself naturally within a short time. If it does not, there are various chemicals you can add to clear it – ask at your nearest water garden specialist or aquarist centre.

(**April**)

Then secure the plant in place by running a length of wire over the rootball and twisting it through the sides of the basket. This is to prevent the plant from floating out while its roots grow into the new compost.

Finally, place a handful or two of clean gravel over the top of the compost to prevent this too from floating out when the basket is submerged. Before planting, water the container well, until the compost is really sloppy. It is now ready for planting in exactly the same way as those bought already prepared from a water garden centre.

Plant standing at the edge of the pond rather than by stepping in, if possible, or there is some risk of cracking the liner. Start at the centre and work your way out.

Plant the waterlily by lowering its container slowly into the centre of the pond. It is essential that the leaves can float on the surface of the water. If the waterlily was previously growing in shallower water than that in your pond, you will find the leaves are pulled down under the water. If this happens, raise the lily container on a brick or upturned flower pot to start with, until its leaves can just float. From then on, each time the plant produces new leaves they will have slightly longer stems, and you can sink the container deeper into the water a little at a time until eventually it is resting on the bottom of the pond.

Just stand the containers of scirpus, iris, acorus and typha in position – these are upright plants whose leaves grow up out of the water, and provided they are planted at approximately the right depth (as shown in the plan) they will not need any special attention at planting time. Hottonia, a floating plant, needs only to be dropped into place in the water.

In subsequent years, divide plants that have become over-large. Lift the baskets out of the water and remove the plants. Divide the roots by tearing the clumps apart and replant the best piece in new compost in the same basket. Treat the divisions as described earlier for planting new plants in baskets.

Every few years, when the pond has become badly overgrown and in need of a spring-clean, remove all the plants, fish and water and scrub out the pond liner with clean water (don't use detergents as they may harm the plants or the fish). Refill with clean water and replant as before. Very occasionally you may need to take everything out to replace a cracked liner – the plastic slowly degrades and the pond starts to leak. When you find yourself refilling the pond very frequently (after about ten years) this is probably the case.

(April)

If you want to put fish in your water garden, add some submerged water plants such as *Elodea crispa* or *Ceratophyllum demersum* for extra oxygenation. (The foliage of hottonia grows under water and also acts as an oxygenator.) They remain under water all the time, giving a vague impression of massed green foliage in the bottom of the pond. They are normally supplied with weights attached, and can be placed into the pond near the centre. You do not need to put them in pots.

Allow at least three weeks after planting the pond before introducing the fish. Buy only healthy fish from a reputable source; avoid any that are sluggish or have white spots on them. Bring them home in plastic bags full of water, tied at the neck, and float the bags in the pond for several hours before releasing them. This is to allow them to acclimatize slowly to the change in water temperature. Remember to feed the fish regularly during the summer – the dealer should recommend the best food.

May

Plant the azolla and eichhornia after the danger of frost has passed by dropping them into place in the water.

> **In subsequent years**, replant azolla and eichhornia as described for the hottonia.

June, July, August

Refill the pond whenever the water level drops by more than a few inches. Keep it regularly topped up.

September

Feed the fish well. Remove eichhornia and azolla plants and overwinter them in a bowl of water in a well-lit place indoors. Or scrap the plants and buy new ones next May.

Remove dead leaves from the surface with a net.

Pull the dead flowers and foliage from the waterlily. Remove any dead leaves from the other plants in the pond to keep it free of decaying vegetation.

> **In subsequent years**, thin out the oxygenating plants (hottonia, elodea and ceratophyllum) late in the month to prevent an excessive build-up of vegetation in the pond.

October

Towards the end of the month, cut down the seed heads of iris and typha close to water level.

November–March

Stop feeding the fish. Top the pond up with water.

If the water freezes over, make a hole in the ice by standing a bowl of hot water on top. Don't use a hammer.

Wildlife Pond

The traditional pond contained a mixture of plants designed to make it as ornamental as possible. However, for a wild garden or for a natural feature in a very informal part of a garden, a completely different style of pond is called for. A 'wildlife pond' relies on an informal shape and plenty of native plants both in and out of the water to re-create the untamed look of a natural beauty spot, and provide a habitat for many water-loving creatures.

April

2 *Hottonia palustris* (instead of 3)

1 *Butomus umbellatus*

1 *Meynanthes trifoliata*

5 *Lythrum salicaria*

12 *Cardamine pratensis*

3 *Valeriana officinalis* (valerian)

1 *Hydrocharis morsus-ranae*

1 *Caltha palustris* (marsh marigold)

10 *Myosotis palustris* (water forget-me-not)

5 *Mentha aquatica* (water mint)

You will also need

An asymmetrical pre-formed pond liner with the sides graduated in two stages to provide different depths of water – 6 inches (15cm) and 24 inches (61cm) – when the pond is filled

50 × 2 gal (10 litre) bucketfuls peat or well-rotted garden compost

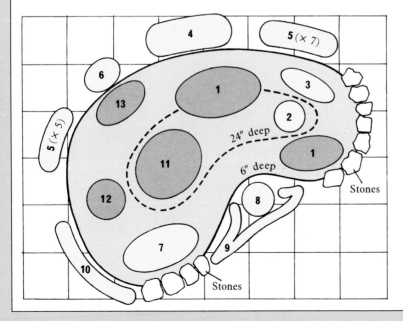

1 *Hottonia* 2 *Butomus*
3 *Meynanthes*: May–June
4 *Lythrum*: June–August
5 *Cardamine*: April–June
6 *Valerian*: June–August
7 *Hydrocharis*: July–August
8 *Marsh marigolds*: April
9 *Water forget-me-nots*: June–July
10 *Water mint*: July–September
11 *Nymphaea* 12 *Typha* 13 *Iris*

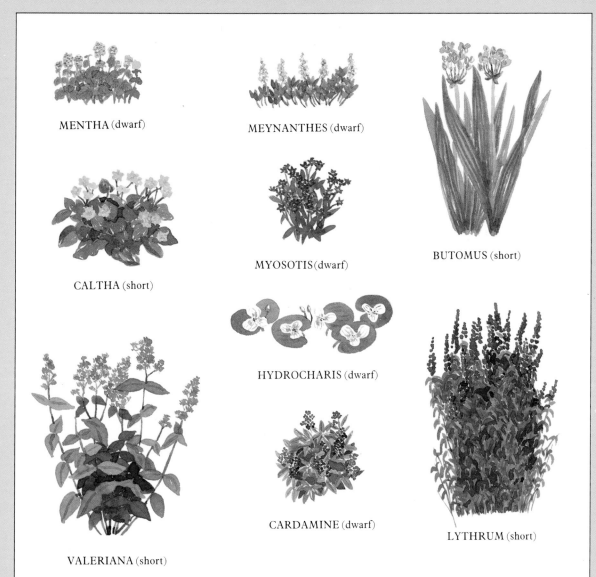

MENTHA (dwarf)

MEYNANTHES (dwarf)

BUTOMUS (short)

CALTHA (short)

MYOSOTIS (dwarf)

HYDROCHARIS (dwarf)

VALERIANA (short)

CARDAMINE (dwarf)

LYTHRUM (short)

Method

Construct the pond as on pages 145 and 146 but this time without putting a complete border of paving round the edge. Instead, sink it slightly deeper into the ground so that the edge of the liner can be concealed under the foliage of surrounding plants, and use a few informally placed pieces of flat rockery stone to complete the edge as shown.

After planting the pond itself (see left) prepare the surroundings. Dig in 2 bucketfuls per sq yd (sq m) of peat or well-rotted garden compost. Do not use manure or fertilizer in case it gets into the pond and turns the water green. Rake the ground roughly level.

Butomus, meynanthes, lythrum, cardamine, valerian, marsh marigolds, water forget-me-nots and water mint are native British plants which can usually be bought from herb farms or wildflower growers; some are also sold through normal garden outlets for planting in borders.

April Hydrocharis is a floating plant and, like the hottonia, should just be dropped into the water in the required place.

Stand the butomus, meynanthes, lythrum, cardamine, valerian, marsh marigolds, water forget-me-nots and water mint out in their planting positions so the leaves of those closest to the pond just overlap the edge of the liner. When you are happy with the positioning, dig holes the same size as the pot, knock the plants out by tapping the base with a trowel and place them into the holes. Firm the soil lightly down round the roots and water the plants in very thoroughly.

If you cannot obtain plants, buy seed instead, available from specialist suppliers. This should be sprinkled thinly on to prepared and raked soil. Rake over the area lightly with the back of the rake and water well.

Replacement and additional plants are given at the start of each variation. For quantities of 'original' plants, uncoloured in the planting plan and not given in the variation ingredients, check with the list at the start of the main plan.

In subsequent years, remove surplus hydrocharis buds.

Some of the marginals (the plants surrounding the pond) may seed themselves and produce lots of seedlings. Leave some of these to grow and increase the natural look of the pond surroundings. Remove any that spread too far or too thickly. Remember, though, a wildlife pond such as this looks more authentic if allowed to become well populated.

May When the seedlings come up after a few weeks, thin them out – you can, if you like, leave more than those shown on the plan so as to 'naturalize' the pond faster. Keep the marginal plants round the edge of the pond very well watered.

September Cut the foliage and dead flower stems of the plants at the water's edge back almost to ground level when they start to die off naturally. Remove the debris from the area, and keep the pond free from decaying vegetation.

Boggy Banks

The first variation used moisture-loving native plants to naturalize the fringes of a wildlife pond. Here the same idea has been adapted to suit a more conventional garden pond, using moisture-loving herbaceous plants with the original 'traditional pond' plants to create a pond with its own bog garden. To the plants in the original list, add the following:

April

4 *Hosta sieboldiana* 'Elegans'

2 *Peltiphyllum peltatum*

1 *Rheum palmatum*

1 *Lobelia fulgens* 'Queen Victoria'

6 *Myosotis palustris* (Water forget-me-not)

2 *Primula japonica*

2 *Astilbe* 'Fanal'

3 *Hakenochloa macro aurea*

1 *Carex stricta aurea*

3 *Cardamine pratensis* 'Flore pleno'

You will also need

A rectangular piece of thick black polythene or butyl pond lining material measuring 20ft × 15ft (6m × 4.5m) (butyl is preferable to polythene as it lasts very much longer before needing to be replaced)

Builder's sand

CAREX (short)

ASTILBE (short)

HAKENOCHLOA (short)

MYOSOTIS (dwarf)

RHEUM (short)   CARDAMINE (dwarf)   HOSTA (dwarf)

PRIMULA(short)

LOBELIA(short)

PELTIPHYLLUM (short)

Method

The method of pond construction used here is very different to that for a conventional pond. There is no well-defined edge to this pond; instead, it merges gently into the surrounding bog garden which is kept permanently moist with water overflowing from the pond.

Start by clearing the area of weeds and digging the soil. Do not add any manure, compost or peat. Rake the soil roughly level and use the point of a stick to mark out the shape of the pond and the plant area surrounding it, as shown on the plan.

Then dig out the soil. Begin with the pond – the centre should be 24 inches (61cm) deep for the waterlily, and the edges 6 inches (15cm) deep for the shallow-water plants. Make the edges of the pond at normal ground level, or only 1 inch (2.5cm) below it. Check as you work to see that the edges of the pond are reasonably level, using the timber and spirit level method described on page 146.

Then continue the excavation outside the pond to form the shapes of the spaces allocated for the surrounding plants. These should be about 9 inches (23cm) deep. Do not worry about excavating the entire area where the rhubarb is to go – just taper the dug-out area away into that corner.

Leave a reasonably flat surface when you finish the digging, and check there are no stones protruding from the soil. Then spread a layer of builder's sand 1–2 inches (2.5–5cm) deep over the area which will be occupied by the pond. There is no need to do this for the surrounding garden area.

Next lay the plastic or butyl sheet over the area so that it overlaps the pond by roughly equal amounts in all directions. It should also completely cover all of the planting areas.

Run a little water into the pool with the hose. As the pond begins to fill, you will see that the sheet is slowly pulled to the centre by the weight of water as it takes up the shape of the pond. If the sheet is drawn too far to one side, exposing part of the planting area, pull it carefully back over. You may need to reposition the sheet slightly in this way several times before it is right. When it seems to be correct fill the pond completely.

Use part of the topsoil that was excavated, mixed with a few bucketfuls of peat, to fill in the pockets in the liner round the edge of the pond where plants are to go, so creating the bog garden.

Use a sharp knife to trim away the surplus lining sheet from round the edges of the area, and dig the edges into the ground to hide them.

Now take a sharp skewer and perforate the liner every 6–12 inches (15–30cm) over the area of the bog garden. This is to provide some slight drainage, leaving the soil at just the right degree of bogginess.

When you have done this, run some more water into the pond. Keep filling until it overflows the edges, flooding into the bog garden areas.

Finally, place some paving stones in position round the edge of the pond at the positions shown on the plan. The garden is now ready for planting.

April   Plant the pond first, following the method described on pages 147 and 148. Work standing on the stones at the side of the pond, so as to avoid either stepping in it (when you risk tearing the lining sheet), or treading in the bog garden round the edge.

Plant the edges of the pond afterwards. Stand the hosta, peltiphyllum, rheum, lobelia, water forget-me-not, primula, astilbe, hakenochloa, carex and cardamine in position, and make a hole for each one big enough to take its rootball. Knock the plants out of their pots by giving the base a sharp tap with the trowel, or cut them away if they are the black plastic bag type, and plant them into the holes. Firm gently round the roots, and water each plant individually to settle the soil round them.

Check every week to see that the bog garden is wet enough and replenish the pond with water whenever the level starts to drop to ensure the garden is kept topped up too.

Do not use slug pellets in the bog garden. Hostas are the plants most susceptible to slugs, though lobelia and astilbe are quite attractive to them too. They can, however, be protected by using slug pellets in the rest of the garden, so preventing slugs from reaching the pond. It is also worth searching for slugs in the area and picking them up by hand. Birds and hedgehogs coming to drink at the pool will do a good job of clearing slugs.

May   Cut down the flower stems of peltiphyllum, cardamine and primula as soon as the flowers are over.

Check every week that the bog garden is wet, and keep the water level in the pond topped up.

June, July, August   Continue checking the bog garden for wetness, and top up the water level when necessary.

September   Cut down the old flower stems and foliage of water forget-me-not, astilbe and hosta, and the foliage of hakenochloa and primula when the plants start to die back.

October   Cut down the old leaves and flowers of rhubarb when they have started to die away naturally. In cold areas, cover the roots with a thick layer of peat or bracken for the winter.

Cut down the old leaves of peltiphyllum when they start to die back naturally, after making the most of their brilliant autumn colouring.

Cut down the old flower stems and foliage of lobelia and carex when the flowers are finished and the plant starts to die back naturally.

1. *Hostas*: July–August
2. *Peltiphyllum*: April
3. *Rheum*: June
4. *Lobelia*: August–end October
5. *Water forget-me-nots*: June–July
6. *Primulas*: May–July
7. *Astilbes*: June–August   8. *Hakenochloa*
9. *Carex*   10. *Cardamine*: April–June
11. *Iris*   12. *Azolla*   13. *Hottonia*
14. *Nymphaea*   15. *Typha*   16. *Acorus*
17. *Eichhornia*   18. *Scirpus*

Circular Pond

This variation is for a very formal water feature and would suit a small town garden or provide a focal point in a semi-formal garden. It makes use of the same range of plants in the main plan, but to strikingly different effect. You will not need eichhornia and azolla.

You will also need

An ornamental stone cherub or other statuary on a plinth for the centre of the pond

Some bricks and cement to complete the edging

A pre-formed liner which provides a depth of 6 inches (15cm) (which may, in a deeper pool, be made by raised shelves or platforms where the plants are to go) and an area 24 inches (61cm) deep for the waterlily

1 *Nymphaea*   **2** *Typha*   **3** *Hottonia*
4 *Cherub*   **5** *Acorus*   **6** *Iris*
7 *Scirpus*

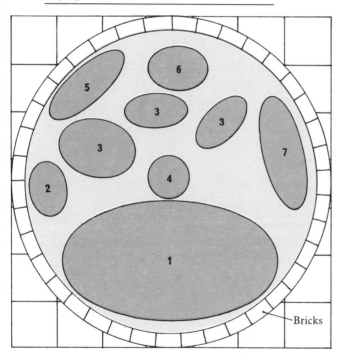

Bricks

Method

Construct the pond following the instructions on pages 145 and 146 and finish it off by building a raised brick surround, one brick high, all round the pond to hide the liner and provide a formal edging. Maintenance and planting are as described in the main plan on pages 147 to 149.

Pond for Fish

The final variation is designed to provide a natural, healthy environment for fish that also looks attractive to us. It uses lots of oxygenating plants and species with large leaves to give fish shade and security from predators – plus a cosy nursery for their young. Overall, it gives a more informal feel to the rectangular pond in the main plan.

1 *Aponogeton distachyon* (water hawthorn) (replaces *Nymphaea* 'James Brydon')

1 *Myriophyllum spicatum*

1 *Potamogeton crispus*

3 *Mimulus luteus* (replace *Typha minima*)

5 *Ranunculus aquatilis* (water crowfoot) (replace *Acorus gramineus* 'Variegata')

1 *Cyperus longus* (replaces *Scirpus tabernaemonti zebrina*)

3 *Pontederia cordata* (pickerel) (replace *Eichhornia crassipes*)

MYRIOPHYLLUM
(dwarf)

CYPERUS (short)

PONTEDERIA
(short)

POTAMOGETON
(dwarf)

MIMULUS (short)

RANUNCULUS
(dwarf)

APONOGETON (dwarf)

Method

Construct and plant the pond as described in the original plan on page 145.

Do not introduce the fish for at least three weeks after planting the pond, to give the plants time to establish. In selecting the fish choose brightly coloured species that frequently come to the surface – Koi carp or traditional goldfish – so that they are easily visible. If you wish to add snails to help keep the pond clean (their eggs will provide extra high-protein food for the fish), choose Ramshorn snails or freshwater winkles, which will not feed on your plants.

April to August Remove plant debris that falls in the pond, or dead leaves and flowers of water plants growing in it. Take care lawn clippings etc do not get into the pond; decomposing vegetation produces gases which are harmful to fish. Do not use weedkillers or fertilizers near the pond, and take care not to use them anywhere in the garden on windy days as even minute quantities blown into the water may also be harmful.

In subsequent years, thin out excess growth of myriophyllum and potamogeton, and remove superfluous self-sown seedlings of aponogeton.

September Take particular care to remove dead foliage and flowers from the pond and remove fallen leaves. Protect the pond by covering it with a net, if necessary.

15-20″ deep | 12″ deep | 6″ deep

1 *Aponogeton* May–October
2 *Myriophyllum*
3 *Potamogeton*
4 *Mimulus*: June
5 *Ranunculus*: May
6 *Cyperus*: August
7 *Hottonia*
8 *Pontederia*: August–September
9 *Iris*

Woodland Gardens

'Wild' gardens have recently become very popular and if you have an area of woodland clearing you are already halfway there. By selecting plants that enjoy the conditions and arranging them informally you can achieve a 'garden' that looks as if it grew naturally. The main plan is for a 'wild' garden in a woodland clearing with a light tree canopy and slightly dry soil. The variations give planting schemes for other soil types. Very little pruning or attention is necessary in these gardens.

Ingredients for a clearing 20ft × 10ft (6m × 3m)

April

12 *Epimedium* × *rubrum*

3 *Alchemilla mollis*

4 *Arundinaria murielae* (bamboo)

1 *Sambucus racemosa* 'Plumosa Aurea'

3 *Berberis* 'Atropurpurea'

1 *Mahonia aquifolium*

8 *Hedera hibernica*

September

24 *Anemone blanda*

From the garden shed

18 × 2 gal (10 litre) bucketfuls of peat or well-rotted garden compost or manure

45oz (1.2kg) of Growmore fertilizer

44 × 2 gal (10 litre) bucketfuls of bark chippings, peat or well-rotted garden compost or leafmould for mulching (optional)

Few lengths of fallen tree or logs

Tools required

Spade

Fork

Mattock (optional)

Rake

Hand trowel

Watering can or hose

Garden line or 4 canes and string

SAMBUCUS (tall)

HEDERA (dwarf)

ARUNDINARIA (tall)

BERBERIS (medium)

MAHONIA (medium)

ALCHEMILLA (short)

EPIMEDIUM (dwarf)

ANEMONE (dwarf)

Method

The method of preparing the soil is rather different for a woodland garden than for a normal garden bed.

Start by clearing any undergrowth such as brambles, nettles, tree seedlings etc from the area, but leave all the existing trees and saplings surrounding it. Do not remove any of the natural leaf litter.

Mark the boundary of the 'bed' out with a garden line or four canes and a piece of string. Then divide the area into squares measuring a yard (1m) each way, using the point of a stick to leave a slight impression in the soil. This gives a guide for marking the positions where the plants are to go. Push a short piece of cane in place for each plant. Then remove the line.

Do not cut an edge round the garden, as this is to be an informal garden, in which the plants are grown 'naturalized' into the surrounding woodland. As the plants grow they will soften the edges of the basic rectangular shape, and blend gently into surrounding trees.

After marking the planting positions, place a few fallen logs to outline the pathway through the clearing, as shown on the plan overleaf.

Prepare the soil where alchemilla, epimedium and hedera are to go by spreading 2 bucketfuls per sq yd (sq m) of peat, compost or manure and forking it into the top few inches of soil. It will be difficult to go deeper than this because of the tree roots you will almost certainly find there. Follow this up by sprinkling Growmore evenly over the area at 4oz (100g) per sq yd (sq m), and raking the ground roughly level.

It is not necessary to prepare the entire area of ground where the mahonia, berberis, arundinaria, and sambucus are to go as is normally done for a traditional bed. Here it will be sufficient to prepare the soil at each planting position, and leave the ground between as it is.

April

Before planting Stand the mahonia, berberis, bamboo and sambucus next to the canes that mark their positions and have ready one bucketful of peat or well-rotted manure or garden compost and 1oz (25g) of Growmore fertilizer for each plant. Mix the two together so that the fertilizer is evenly distributed throughout.

Planting Dig holes in the positions marked by the canes, about twice the size of the roots of the plant that is to go into each one. Pile the soil you dig out into a heap alongside each hole. Fork over the soil at the bottom of the hole to loosen it and tip in half the bucketful of compost and fertilizer mixture. Stir this

MAINTENANCE

Mulch the entire area by spreading a thin layer of bark chippings, peat, or well-rotted garden compost or leafmould over the soil surface. Alternatively, if there is sufficient natural leafmould and litter available in the woodland surrounding your clearing this could be used instead. The path between the plants should also be covered with the mulching material. This is partly to prevent weeds from coming up and partly to complete the natural look of the surface.

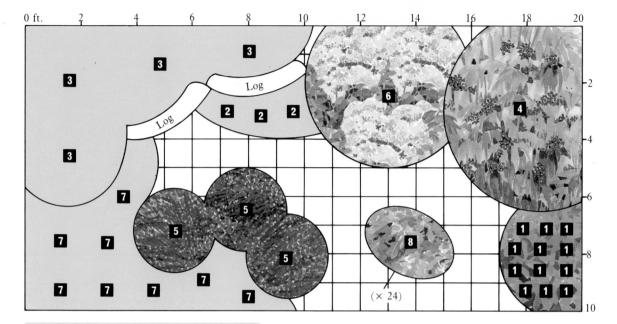

The following scale markings appear at the top of the plan:

0 ft.   2   4   6   8   10   12   14   16   18   20

(× 24)

round with a fork to mix it into the loose soil at the bottom of the hole. Add the remaining mixture in the bucket to the heap of soil at the side of the hole and mix them together. This will be used for filling in round the roots when you plant.

To knock plants out of rigid containers, just tap the base with the back of the trowel first. The kind of containers that are like black polythene bags should be carefully cut away without damaging the ball of roots inside.

Stand the rootballs of the mahonia, berberis, bamboo and sambucus in the centre of the holes you have made. Place a short piece of cane over the hole to see if the top of the rootball is level with the surrounding soil. If it is not, then either remove soil from the bottom of the hole or add some from the pile alongside it until the top is level.

Then fill in round the roots with the rest of the soil/compost mixture. Firm gently down round the plant with your foot to consolidate the soil slightly.

Plant the alchemilla, epimedium and hedera by digging a hole the same

Opposite   Woodland garden.   **Above**   Plan for the garden.   Coloured areas indicate plants in flower in spring. Average flowering periods are listed below:
1 *Epimedium*: May   **2** *Alchemilla*: June–August
3 *Arundinaria*   **4** *Sambucus*: Berries June–July
5 *Berberis*: Foliage May–August   **6** *Mahonia*: March–April   **7** *Hedera*   **8** *Anemones*:February–April

In subsequent years, dig up and divide clumps of bamboo when the old plants start to become too big – this will be quite a major undertaking as the roots become very densely matted together. A mattock is the implement traditionally used for dividing bamboos, but if you do not happen to have one try using two strong garden forks back to back instead, aided by an old bow saw or a large knife to help cut through the root mass. Replant those sections of roots with plenty of new young growth from round the outside of the original clump.

Alchemilla may also be divided when the clumps start to grow large and elderly.

Prune mahonia, berberis and sambucus only to remove dead, frost-damaged or misshapen branches. Cut these right back to a natural junction with another branch.

Cut back hedera if it starts to become too invasive but, ideally, it should be encouraged to spread out of the garden and into the neighbouring woodland.

(April)

size as the pot and fitting the rootball into it. Make sure the top of the rootball is level with the surrounding soil. Fill in round the roots with soil and firm it down with the handle of the trowel.

Water the plants to settle the soil round the roots. Give the mahonia, berberis, bamboo and sambucus about 1 gal (4.5 litres) of water each, and the alchemilla, epimedium and hedera about 2pts (1 litre) each.

May, June, July, August

Water the new plants whenever the soil round them feels dry. Check every week and water as often as necessary. This will help the plants to become well established and start them growing quickly. You will probably find that plants in a woodland need more water than those in a border to start with; the trees will take a great deal of water from the soil, which will consequently dry out faster than normal.

Weed whenever necessary, though the combination of natural shade plus the mulch will be sufficient to prevent most normal annual weed seeds from germinating.

Strong-growing perennial weeds such as nettles and brambles may be a problem, however. Paint the leaves with Glyphosate gel or dab them with a touch weeder (the kind sold for spot treating daisies in lawns) as soon as they appear. If they have been allowed to become large, cut them off at ground level and paint the new growth when it appears. This avoids disturbing the plants they are growing among and is also much easier than trying to dig them out of ground filled with tree roots. Do make sure not to let either weedkiller get on to the leaves of the cultivated plants. If this does happen, wash the leaves thoroughly with water.

September

Plant the anemone corms by digging a hole 3 inches (7.5cm) deep and dropping a corm into the bottom of each – do not worry about getting them the right way up as it is not possible to tell which it is. Fill the holes in with soil.

Cut down the dead flower stems and old foliage of alchemilla, but leave the new foliage growing at the centre of the plant.

Acid Soil

Acid soil should not be regarded as a problem but as the means of growing a huge range of exotic and colourful acid-loving plants such as camellias and rhododendrons. This variation uses the same design as before, but substitutes plants appropriate to the soil conditions.

April

1 *Camellia* 'Donation' (replaces *Sambucus racemosa* 'Plumosa Aurea')

4 *Rhododendron yakushimanum* (replace *Arundinaria murielae*)

3 *Pernettya mucronata* 'Bell's Seedling' (replace *Berberis* 'Atropurpurea')

1 *Fothergilla major* (replaces *Mahonia aquifolium*)

1 *Pieris japonica* 'Variegata' (replaces *Epimedium* × *rubrum*)

4 *Gaultheria procumbens* (replace *Alchemilla mollis* and *Anemone blanda*)

28 *Pachysandra terminalis* 'Variegata' (replace *Hedera hibernica*)

PERNETTYA (medium)

RHODODENDRON (short)

CAMELLIA (tall)

GAULTHERIA (short)

PIERIS (medium)

FOTHERGILLA (medium)

PACHYSANDRA (dwarf)

Method

Before planting it is a good idea to check your soil to see that it really is sufficiently acid. Either send a sample off for analysis (the public analyst, contactable via the local council, may be able to arrange this, or will put you in touch with someone who can), or buy a soil test kit and do it yourself.

When gathering soil for analysis, either at home or at a laboratory, it is very important to make sure the sample is truly representative of the area to be planted. It commonly happens that soil analysis produces misleading results when the soil is all taken from one place. To collect a good sample, take a trowel and a large plastic bag and dig a series of holes to the full depth of the trowel all over the area to be planted, about 2yds (1.8m) apart. Scoop a small sample of soil from the bottom of each hole and mix all the samples together in the plastic bag. Remove a small quantity to test.

To grow the acid-loving plants in this plan, you will need a soil with a pH of 4.5–6.5. At pH 6.5, soil is described as only slightly acid. In this case it may be advisable to use moss peat, which is itself acid, to increase the acidity of the soil when planting instead of manure or compost.

April Plant the camellia, rhododendrons, pernettya, fothergilla, pieris, gaultheria and pachysandra following the instructions on page 162.

In subsequent years, mulch round rhododendron, pieris and camellia by spreading moist moss peat round each trunk, extending as far as the canopy of leaves.

Pruning is not generally necessary other than to remove any dead or damaged branches.

May Weed and water following the instructions on page 164.

Replacement and additional plants are given at the start of each variation. For quantities of 'original' plants, uncoloured in the planting plan and not given in the variation ingredients, check with the list at the start of the main plan.

In subsequent years, deadhead rhododendron and camellia by nipping off the dead flowerheads between thumb and forefinger rather than with secateurs. This is because the new shoots that will carry next year's flowers grow out from just below the old flower heads and they are easily cut off by mistake with secateurs.

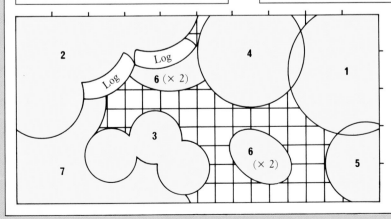

1 *Camellia*: November–April
2 *Rhododendrons*: May–June
3 *Pernettya*: May–early June
4 *Fothergilla*: May
5 *Pieris*: April–May
6 *Gaultheria*: July–August
7 *Pachysandra*: February–March

Alkaline Soil

This variation is for a different kind of 'problem' soil – this time alkaline, which gardeners usually describe as chalky, though chalk is not always apparent. Do not attempt to alter the pH of your soil if it is naturally acid.

April

1 *Daphne mezereum* 'Grandiflorum' (replaces *Epimedium* × *rubrum*)

COTONEASTER (tall)

April Prepare the ground and plant the daphne, euonymus and cotoneaster following the instructions for mahonia etc on page 162.

4 *Euonymus fortunei* 'Emerald 'n' Gold' (replace *Alchemilla mollis* and *Anemone blanda*)

3 *Cotoneaster conspicuus* (replace *Berberis* 'Atropurpurea')

EUONYMUS (short)   DAPHNE (short)

In subsequent years, prune cotoneaster if the plants get too big by reducing the length of overlong branches. Do the same if the plants grow out of shape – this cotoneaster should resemble a cascade of branches.

Daphne is very slow growing and the only pruning that will be needed is if any branches die back. Cut back to a natural joint with a well-shaped, healthy branch.

1 *Euonymus*
2 *Cotoneaster*: September–October
3 *Daphne*: February–April
4 *Sambucus*   5 *Hedera*
6 *Arundinaria*   7 *Mahonia*

Damp Soil

This 'problem' soil is the best kind for a woodland garden, and the variation takes advantage of this to create a damp, shady garden that will provide a range of colour all year round.

April

5 *Primula japonica* (replace *Alchemilla mollis*)

1 *Gunnera manicata* (replaces 3 *Arundinaria murielae*)

1 *Acer palmatum* 'Atropurpureum', 3 *Hosta fortunei* 'Albopicta', and 5 *Primula vialii*
      replace *Berberis*

1 *Viburnum rhytidophyllum* (replaces *Mahonia aquifolium*)

3 *Peltiphyllum peltatum* (replace 1 *Arundinaria murielae*)

September

24 *Galanthus nivalis* (snowdrops) and 12 *Erythronium dens-canis*
      (replace *Anemone blanda*)

ACER (medium)

VIBURNUM (tall)

GUNNERA (tall)

HOSTA (short)

ERYTHRONIUM (short)

PRIMULA VIALII (short)

PELTIPHYLLUM (short)

PRIMULA JAPONICA (short)

GALANTHUS (dwarf)

April Plant out the primulas, gunnera, hosta and peltiphyllum following the instructions for alchemilla etc on page 163. Plant acer and viburnum following instructions for mahonia etc on page 162.

September Plant the snowdrop and erythronium bulbs in clumps of two, three or four over the area allocated to them for a nice natural effect. Dig out individual holes, which should be approximately $2\frac{1}{2}$ times as deep as the bulb itself. Put a little peat or compost at the bottom of the hole and plant by pressing each bulb gently into it. Then fill the hole in with soil or a mixture of soil and peat.

In subsequent years, allow the dead flower heads to remain on *Primula japonica* so it can set seed. These will fall and should grow into new plants without any intervention. Dig up the seedlings and replant in the correct position to replace the parents.

June Cut down the flower stems of peltiphyllum when the flowers are over.

July Cut down the flower stems of primula as soon as the flowers are over.

Towards the end of the month, cut down the old foliage of hosta when it starts to die back naturally.

October Cut down the old leaves and flowers of gunnera when they have started to die away naturally. In cold areas, cover the roots with a thick layer of peat or bracken for the winter.

Cut down the old leaves of peltiphyllum when they start to die back naturally, after making the most of their brilliant autumn colouring.

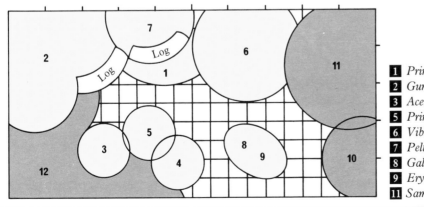

1 *Primula japonica*: May–July
2 *Gunnera*: April–October
3 *Acer*   4 *Hostas*: July
5 *Primula vialli*: June–July
6 *Viburnum*: May–June
7 *Peltiphyllum*: April
8 *Galanthus*: January–March
9 *Erythronium*   10 *Epimedium*
11 *Sambucus*   12 *Hedera*

Wildflower Garden

Conventional shrubs and ground cover plants are omitted from this variation and replaced with wild flowers, bought as plants or seeds, to create an authentic woodland clearing.

March

3 *Dipsacus fullonum* (teasel) (replace *Epimedium × rubrum*)

5 *Primula elatior* (oxslip) (replace *Alchemilla mollis*)

12 *Digitalis purpurea* (foxglove) (replace *Arundinaria murielae*)

3 *Silene dioica* (red campion) and
12 *Stellaria holostea* (greater stitchwort) replace *Berberis*

6 *Viola riviniana* (violet) and
6 *Fragaria vesca* (wild strawberry) (replace *Anemone blanda*)

12 *Epilobium angustifolium* (rose bay willow herb) (replace *Mahonia aquifolium* and *Sambucus racemosa* 'Plumosa Aurea')

24 *Endymion non-scriptus* (bluebells) (replace *Hedera hibernica*)

DIPSACUS (medium)

PRIMULA (short)

SILENE (short)

DIGITALIS (medium)

EPILOBIUM (medium)

STELLARIA (short)

VIOLA (dwarf)

FRAGARIA (dwarf)

ENDYMION (dwarf)

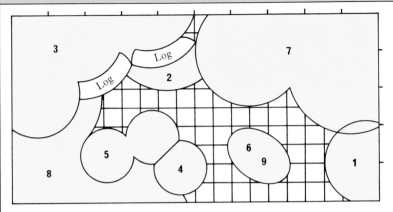

1 *Dipsacus*: July–August
2 *Primulas*: March–May
3 Foxgloves: July–September
4 *Silene*: April–June
5 *Stellaria*: April–June
6 *Violets*: March–May
7 *Epilobium*: June–September
8 *Bluebells*: April–June
9 *Fragaria*

March If you buy plants, mark out the ground and planting positions as suggested in the original plan. Dig a hole twice the size of each plant's root-ball and mix a spadeful of peat or compost into the bottom. Use a mixture of soil and compost or peat to fill in round the roots, as on page 163.

If you buy seeds, clear the ground of weeds and debris and roughly fork compost into the top 3–4 inches (7–10cm); use the same total quantity as stated in our original plan. Rake the ground level, and scatter the seed.

Rake over the same ground again, but very lightly this time so as to just cover the seeds with soil. Then water, and leave well alone.

September, October To plant the bluebells, dig a hole three times the depth of each 'bulb' and drop a handful of compost into the bottom. Then press the bluebell firmly into it before filling the hole with a mixture of soil and compost.

In subsequent years, replace dipsacus with new plants, as they are biennial and die after flowering. You should only need to replace them once, as in following years the original plants will have seeded and self-sown seedlings will appear. This will also happen with the other wildflowers you have introduced, so that they gradually naturalize the whole area; any that come up where you do not want them can however be pulled out.

April, May If the seedlings look crowded when they emerge, thin them by pulling out the weakest-looking ones. Otherwise nothing further is necessary.

Late in September, cut down the dead flower stems of digitalis and epilobium. Leave the teasels of dipsacus as winter ornamentation.

Index

Page numbers in *italics* refer to captions to plans.

A

Abies koreana, 94, 102; *97, 103*
Acanthus mollis, 26, 37; *28, 34, 37*
Acer palmatum 'Atropurpureum', 168; *169*
Achillea 'Galaxy Hybrids', 20
Acorus gramineus 'Variegatus', 144; *146, 156*
African lily see *Agapanthus*
Agapanthus 'Headbourne Hybrid', 66; *68, 74, 76, 78, 80*
Ajuga reptans, 31, 123, 127; *32, 124, 128*
A.r. 'Atropurpurea', 16, 18; *17, 19*
Alchemilla mollis, 16, 18, 20, 26, 50, 63, 66, 123, 160; *17, 19, 21, 28, 36, 37, 53, 60, 65, 68, 74, 76, 78, 80, 124, 163*
Allium schoenoprasum, 38, 43, 44, 48, 79; *40, 43, 45, 47, 48, 80*
Althaea rosea, 50; *53*
Amaranthus caudatus, 132; *135, 138, 139, 141*
A.c. 'Viridis', 137, 138; *138, 139*
Anaphalis triplinervis, 20, 31, 33, 73; *21, 32, 34, 74*
Anemone blanda, 77, 160; *78, 124, 163*
A. × hybrida, 63; *65*
angelica see *Angelica archangelica*
Angelica archangelica, 44, 46, 79; *45, 47, 80*
annuals, dry sunny beds, 129–31
Anthemis tinctoria 'Grallagh Gold', 46; *47*
Antirrhinum 'Floral Carpet', 8; *11*
Aponogeton distachyon, 157; *158*
apple mint see *Mentha rotundifolia*
Aquilegia 'McKana Hybrids', 8, 63; *21, 24, 65*
Armeria maritima, 8, 22, 33, 66; *11, 24, 34, 68, 74, 78*
Aruncus sylvester, 18; *19*
Arundinaria murielae, 160; *163, 167*
Aster × frikartii, 61; *62*
A. novi-belgii, 35, 50; *36, 53*
Astilbe × arendsii 'Fanal', 8; *11, 17, 19, 21, 153, 155*

Astrantia maxima, 20, 33; *21, 34*
avens see *Geum*
Azalea 'Elizabeth', 104; *106, 110*
A. mollis, 66; *68, 76*
Azolla filiculoides, 144; *155*

B

baby's breath see *Gypsophila*
bamboo see *Arundinaria*
barberry see *Berberis*
basil see *Ocimum basilicum* and *O. purpurea*
bay see *Laurus nobilis*
bear's breeches see *Acanthus mollis*
Begonia semperflorens, 66; *68, 74, 80*
bellflower see *Campanula*
Berberis darwinii, 104; *106, 110*
B. thunbergii 'Atropurpurea', 123, 125; *124, 160; 163*
B.t. 'Rose Glow', 66; *68, 78, 80*
bergamot see *Monarda didyma*
Bergenia 'Ballawley Hybrids', 18, 22, 33, 35, 66, 123; *19, 34, 36, 68, 74, 78, 124, 126*
bishop's hat see *Epimedium × rubra*
bleeding hearts see *Dicentra spectabilis*
blue and white borders, 31–3
box see *Buxus sempervirens suffruticosa*
broom see *Cytisus*
Buddleia davidii, 115; *116*
bugle see *Ajuga reptans*
bulbs, paved areas, 77–8
busy Lizzie see *Impatiens*
Butomus umbellatus, 150; *150*
butterfly bush see *Buddleia davidii*
Buxus sempervirens suffruticosa, 43; *43*

C

Caltha palustris, 150; *150*
Camellia × williamsii 'Donation', 66, 165; *68, 74, 76, 78, 80, 166*
Campanula carpatica 'Jingle Bells', 26, 73; *28, 36, 37, 74*
C. lactiflora, 73; *74*
C. medium, 50; *53, 60*
C.m. 'Calycanthema', 31; *32*
candytuft see *Iberis*
Canterbury bell see *Campanula medium*

Cardimine pratensis, 150, 153; *150, 155*
C.p. 'Flore Pleno', 153
Carex stricta aurea, 153; *155*
catmint see *Nepeta*
cedar see *Cedrus*
Cedrus libani 'Sargentii', 100; *100*
Ceratophyllum demersum, 144
Chaenomeles speciosa, 115; *116*
Chamaecyparis lawsoniana 'Ellwoodii' 100, 102; *100, 103*
C. obtusa 'Nana Gracilis', 94, 96, 100, 102; *97, 100, 103*
C.o. 'Tetragona Aurea', 99; *99*
C. pisifera 'Boulevard', 75, 94; *76, 9̶*
C.p. 'Filifera Aurea', 75, 99; *76, 99*
Chinese witch hazel see *Hamamellis*
Chionodoxa luciliae, 77; *78*
chives see *Allium schoenoprasum*
Chrysanthemum maximum, 31, 33, 35; *32, 34, 36*
Clematis montana, 50; *53*
Coleus blumei, 140; *141*
columbine see *Aquilegia*
conifer beds, 94–103
    dwarf, 101
    emphasis on form, 100
    golden, 99
    with ground cover, 102–3
    ingredients, 94
    maintenance, 96–8
    planting, 96
containers, herbs, 48–9
Convallaria majalis, 63; *65*
coral flower see *Heuchera sanguinea*
Coreopsis verticillata, 26, 37; *28, 36, 37*
cornel see *Cornus alba*
Cornus alba 'Elegantissima', 109, 111 *110, 112*
Cosmos bipinnatus 'Sensation Mixed', 138; *139*
Continus coggygria, 109, 111; *110, 11̶*
Cotoneaster conspicuus, 167; *167*
C.c. 'Decorus', 123; *124*
C. horizontalis, 102, 104; *103, 106, 110*
cottage garden borders, 50–65
    cut flowers, 61–2
    ingredients, 50

maintenance, 52–5
planting, 52
scented borders, 56–8
shady areas, 63–5
traditional borders, 59–60
cranesbill *see Geranium*
cuckoo flower *see Cardamine pratensis*
cushion spurge *see Euphorbia polychroma*
Cyperus longus, 157; *158*
cypress *see Chamaecyparis*
Cytisus × *kewensis*, 109, 113; *110, 114*

D
daffodil *see Narcissus*
damask violet *see Hesperis matronalis*
dame's violet see Hesperis matronalis
Daphne mezereum 'Grandiflorum', 167; *167*
  D. odora, 113; *114*
  D.o 'Aureomarginata', 115; *116*
day lilies *see Hemerocallis*
Delphinium 'Pacific Hybrids', 8, 26, 50; *11, 17, 21, 28, 36, 37, 53, 62*
Dianthus 'Doris', 8, 33, 61, 66, 118; *11, 17, 21, 24, 34, 62, 121, 128*
  D. 'Mrs Sinkins', 31, 50; *32, 53, 57, 60, 68, 74, 78, 80*
Dicentra spectabilis, 59; *60*
Digitalis purpurea, 170; *171*
  D.p. 'Excelsior Hybrids', 8, 59, 63; *11, 17, 19, 60, 65*
dill *see Peucedanum graveolens*
Dipsacus fullorum, 170; *171*
dog's-tooth violet *see Erythronium denscanis*
dry beds, 118–31
  with annuals, 129–31
  ingredients, 118
  island beds, 127–8
  maintenance, 120–2
  planting, 120
  shady borders, 125–6
dwarf conifers, 101

E
Eichhornia crassipes, 144; *155*
Elaeagnus pungens 'Maculata', 66, 111, 123; *68, 76, 112, 124*
Elodea crispa, 144
Endymion non-scriptus, 170; *171*
Epilobium angustifolium, 170; *171*
Epimedium × *rubrum*, 160; *163, 169*
Erica carnea 'Pink Spangles', 102; *103*
  E.c. 'Springwood White', 102; *103*

Erythronium dens-canis, 168; *169*
Euonymus fortunei 'Emerald 'n' Gold', 18, 66, 109, 111, 167; *19, 68, 74, 76, 78, 80, 110, 112, 167*
  E.f. 'Silver Queen', 111, 125; *112, 126*
evergreen plants:
  conifer beds, 94–103
  paved areas, 75–6
everlasting pea *see Lathyrus latifolius*

F
fences, beds bordering, 37–8
fennel *see Foeniculum vulgare*
floating water hyacinth *see Eichhornia crassipes*
flower arrangers, mixed borders for, 20–1
flowering rush *see Butomus sempervirens*
Foeniculum vulgare, 38, 44; *40, 45*
foliage, summer borders, 140–1
forget-me-not *see Myosotis*
Forsythia × *intermedia* 'Spectabilis', 113; *114*
Fothergilla major, 165; *166*
foxglove *see Digitalis purpurea*
Fragaria vesca, 170; *171*
French sorrel *see Rumex scutatus*

G
Galanthus nivalis, 77, 168; *78, 169*
Gaultheria procumbens, 165; *166*
gay feather *see Liastris*
Genista lydia, 102, 104, 113; *103, 106, 110, 114*
geranium *see Geranmium and Pelargonium*
Geranium endressi 'Wargrave Pink', 33, 50; *53*
  G. 'Johnson's Blue', 31, 35, 50, 66; *32, 36, 60, 68, 78*
Geum chiloense 'Mrs Bradshaw', 26; *28*
globe thistle *see Echinops ritro*
glory of the snow *see Chionodoxa luciliae*
goat's beard *see Aruncus sylvester*
Godetia, 66, 138; *68, 78, 80, 139*
golden marguerite *see Anthemis tinctoria*
golden marjoram *see Origanum vulgare*
grape hyacinth *see Muscari armeniacum*
ground cover:
  conifer beds, 102–3

rose gardens, 88–9
Gunnera manicata, 168; *169*
Gypsophila elegans, 139; *139*
  G. paniculata, 142; *143*
  G.p. 'Bristol Fairy', 20, 26, 73, 75; *21, 28, 34, 36, 37, 74, 76*

H
Hakenochloa macro aurea, 153; *155*
Hamamelis mollis 'Pallida', 113, 115; *114, 116*
heather *see Erica carnea*
Hebe 'Autumn Glory', 109; *110*
  H. 'Great Orme', 109; *110*
Hedera colchica 'Paddy's Pride', 22; *24*
  H. hibernica, 160; *163, 167, 169*
hedges, beds bordering, 37–8
Helianthemum nummularium, 26, 73; *28, 36, 37, 74*
  H.n. 'Wisley Pink', 118; *121, 128*
Helleborus foetidus, 18; *19*
  H. orientalis, 63; *65*
Hemerocallis 'Golden Chimes', 63; *65*
herb gardens, 38–48
  borders, 46–7
  classical, 43
  containers, 48–9
  decorative, 44–5
  paved areas, 79–80
herbaceous beds, 26–36
  blue and white beds, 31–2
  bordering walls, hedges and fences, 37–8
  island beds, 26–36
  longer beds, 35–6
  maintenance, 29–30
  pink and silver beds, 33–5
Hesperis matronalis, 56, 59; *57, 60*
Heuchera sanguinea, 33, 63; *34, 65*
Hibiscus syriacus, 113; *114*
Hinoki cypress *see Chamaecyparis obtusa*
hollyhock *see Althaea rosea*
honeysuckle *see Lonicera*
hop *see Humulus*
Hosta fortunei 'Albopicta', 18, 26, 61, 73, 142, 168; *19, 28, 36, 62, 74, 143, 169*
  H. sieboldiana 'Elegans', 8, 153; *11, 17, 19, 21, 155*
Hottonia palustris, 144, 150, 157; *146, 150, 155, 156, 158*
Humulus japonicus 'Variegatus', 140; *141*
Hydrocharis morus-ranae, 150; *150*
Hypericum 'Hidcote', 113; *114*

I

Iberis 'Giant Hyacinth', 118; *121, 128, 129*
  I. sempervirens, 88; *88*
Impatiens 'Pastel Mixed', 66; *68, 76, 80*
Iris laevigata, 144, 157; *146, 150, 155, 156, 158*
  I. reticulata, 77; *78*
  I. unguicularis, 77; *78*
island beds, 26–36
  blue and white beds, 31–2
  dry sunny beds, 127–8
  longer beds, 35–6
  pink and silver beds, 33–4
ivy *see Hedera*

J

Japanese anemone *see Anemone × hydrida*
Japanese quince *see Chaenomeles speciosa*
Jew's mallow *see Kerria japonica*
juniper *see Juniperus*
Juniperus horizontalis, 75, 100; *100, 101*
  J.h. 'Banff', 127; *128, 129*
  J. sabina 'Tamariscifolia', 94, 101; *97, 101*
  J. squamata 'Blue Star', 75, 101, 118; *76, 101, 121, 126*

K

Kerria japonica 'Pleniflora', 104; *106, 110*
Kniphofia uvaria, 59; *60*
Kochia trichophylla, 140; *141*

L

lady's mantle *see Alchemilla mollis*
lady's smock *see Cardamine pratensis*
Lamium galeobdolon 'Beacon Silver', 88; *88*
Lathyrus latifolius, 59; *60*
  L. odoratus, 8; *11, 21*
  L.o. 'Antique Fantasy Mixed', 50; *53, 57*
  L.o. 'Knee Hi', 142; *143*
  L.o. 'Spencer Mixed', 61; *62*
Laurus nobilis, 44, 46, 48; *45, 47, 48*
Lavandula spica 'Hidcote', 22, 44, 46, 56, 61, 79, 90, 109, 115, 118; *24, 45, 47, 57, 62, 80, 90, 110, 116, 121, 128, 129*
lavender *see Lavandula*
Lawson cypress *see Chamaecyparis*

lawsoniana
lenten rose *see Helleborus orientalis*
Liatris spicata callilepsis, 22; *24*
Ligularia przewalskii, 18; *19*
lilies *see Lilium*
Lilium candidum, 31; *32*
  L. regale, 8, 56, 61, 63; *11, 17, 21, 57, 62*
lily of the valley *see Convallaria majalis*
Liriope muscari, 31
Livingstone daisy *see Mesembryanthemum criniflorum*
Lobelia, 66, 140; *68, 76, 141*
  L. erinus 'Mrs Clibran', 8, 132, 140; *11, 135, 138*
  L. fulgens 'Queen Victoria', 153; *155*
Lonicera fragrantissima, 56; *57*
  L. nitida 'Baggesen's Gold', 75; *76*
  L. periclymenum 'Belgica', 63; *65*
  L.p. 'Serotina', 16, 18, 63; *17, 19, 65*
love-in-a-mist *see Nigella*
love-lies-bleeding *see Amarathus caudatus*
Lupinus 'Russell Hybrids', 16, 26, 35, 50; *17, 28, 36, 37, 53*
Lythrum salicaria, 150; *150*

M

madonna lily *see Lilium candidum*
Mahonia aquifolium, 18, 104, 111, 160; *19, 106, 110, 112, 163, 167*
Malcolmia maritima, 56, 132; *57, 135, 139*
maple *see Acer*
marjoram *see Origanum*
marsh marigold *see Caltha palustris*
Mentha aquatica, 150; *150*
  M. rotundifolia, 38, 43, 46, 48; *40, 43, 47, 48*
  M. spicata, 38, 48; *40*
Mesembryanthemum criniflorum, 22; *24*
  M.c. 'Mixed', 129; *129*
Meynanthes trifoliata, 150; *150*
michaelmas daisy *see Aster*
Mignonette *see Reseda odorata*
Mimulus luteus, 157; *156*
mint *see Mentha*
mixed borders, 8–24
  for flower arrangers, 20–1
  ingredients, 8
  low maintenance borders, 16–17
  maintenance, 10–15
  method, 10
  on poor soil, 22–4
  shady borders, 18–19
mock orange *see Philadelphus*

Monarda didyma 'Croftway Pink', 33, 56; *34, 57*
monkey flower *see Mimulus*
Muscari armeniacum, 77; *78*
Myosotis alpestris 'Blue Ball', 66; *68, 74, 78*
  M. palustris, 150, 153; *150, 155*
Myrophyllum spicatum, 157; *158*
Myrrhis odorata, 44, 46; *45, 47*

N

Narcissus 'Cheerfulness', 77; *78*
  N. 'Jonquil', 77; *78*
  N. triandrus albus, 77; *78*
nasturtium *see Tropaeoleum majus*
Nepeta × faassenii, 16, 26, 31, 56, 73; *17, 28, 32, 36, 37, 57, 74*
New Zealand flax *see Phormium tenax*
Nicotiana alata 'Lime Green', 20, 138; *21*
  N.a. 'Sensation Mixed', 8, 56, 61, 132; *11, 57, 62, 135, 139, 143*
Nigella damascena, 66; *68, 76, 78, 80*
  N.d. 'Miss Jekyll', 132; *135, 138, 143*
Nymphaea 'James Brydon', 144; *146, 150, 155, 156*

O

Ocimum basilicum, 38, 43, 48; *40, 43, 47, 48*
Ocimum purpurea 'Dark Opal', 46; *47*
old-fashioned borders, 50–65
  cut flowers, 61–2
  ingredients, 50
  maintenance, 52–5
  planting, 52
  scented borders, 56–8
  shady areas, 63–5
  traditional borders, 59–60
Oregon grape *see Mahonia aquifolia*
Origanum majorana, 38, 43, 44, 48; *40, 43, 45, 48*
  O. vulgare, 38; *40*
  O.v. 'Aureum', 46, 56, 79; *47, 57, 80*
Osteospermum 'Polestar', 129; *129*
ox-eye chamomile *see Anthemis tinctoria*

P

Pachysandra terminalis 'Variegata', 165; *166*
parsley *see Petroselinum crispum*
paved gardens, 66–80
  bulbs, 77–8

evergreen, 75–6
herbs, 79–80
ingredients, 66
perennial plants, 73–4
pearl everlasting *see Anaphalis triplinervis*
Pelargonium 'Apple Blossom', 66; *68, 76*
  P. 'Rose Diamond', 132; *135, 139, 143*
  P. 'Scarlet Diamond', 137, 140; *138, 141*
Peltiphyllum peltatum, 153, 168; *155, 169*
Pernettya mucronata 'Bell's Seedling', 165; *166*
Perovskia atriplicifolia, 118; *121, 128, 129*
Petroselinum crispum, 38, 43, 44, 46, 48, 79; *40, 43, 45, 47, 48, 80*
Petunia 'Resisto Mixed', 8, 66, 132; *11, 68, 76, 80, 135, 139, 143*
  P. 'Super Cascade Lilac', 138
  P. 'White Magic', 137; *138*
Peucedanum graveolens, 38, 43, 46, 79; *40, 43, 47, 80*
Philadelphus 'Belle Etoile', 113, 115; *114, 116*
Phlox paniculata,
  P.p. 'Chintz', 33, 61; *34, 62*
  P.p. 'Marlborough', 26; *28, 36, 37*
    P.p. 'White Admiral', 31, 142; *32; 143*
Phormium tenax 'Purpureum', 75; *76*
Picea glauca 'Albertiana Concia', 94, 100; *97, 100*
pickerel *see Pontederia cordata*
Pieris japonica 'Variegata', 165; *166*
pink and silver beds, 33–5
pinks *see Dianthus*
Pinus sylvestris 'Beuvronensis', 100, 101; *100, 101*
plantain lily *see Hosta*
Polygonatum multiflorum, 18, 63; *19, 65*
Polygonum affine 'Donald Lowndes', 26, 37, 123, 125, 127; *28, 36, 37, 124, 126, 128*
ponds, 144–58
  boggy banks, 153–5
  circular ponds, 156
  fish ponds, 157–8
  ingredients, 144
  maintenance, 147–9
  planting, 147–9
  wildlife ponds, 150–2

Pontederia cordata, 157; *158*
poor soil, mixed borders for, 22–4
Portulaca grandiflora, 22; *24*
Potamogeton crispus, 157; *158*
Potentilla fruticosa, 109, 113; *110, 114*
Primula elatior, 170; *171*
  P. japonica, 153, 168; *155, 169*
  P. viallii, 168; *169*
  P. vulgaris, 63; *65*
Pulmonaria officinalis, 63; *65*
purple loosestrife *see Lythrum salicaria*
Pyrethrum roseum 'Eileen May Robinson', 33; *34*

R
Ranunculus aquatilis, 157; *158*
red campion *see Silene dioica*
red-hot poker *see Kniphofia*
regal lily *see Lilium regale*
Reseda odorata, 56, 132; *57, 135, 141*
Rheum palmatum, 153; *155*
Rhododendron yakushimanum, 165; *166*
Ricinus communis 'Impala', 140; *141*
rock broom *see Genista lydia*
rock rose *see Helianthemum*
Romneya coulteri, 22; *24*
Rosa 'Alec's Red', 92; *92*
  R. 'Allgold', 82, 93; *84, 88, 93*
  R. 'Baby Darling', 82, 90; *84, 90, 93*
  R. 'Baby Masquerade', 82; *84, 93*
  R. 'Boule de Neige', 115; *116*
  R. 'Chanelle', 92; *92*
  R. 'Chicago Peace', 82; *84, 88, 90, 93*
  R. 'Elegance', 8; *11, 21*
  R. 'Elizabeth of Glamis', 8; *11, 21*
  R. 'English Miss', 92; *92*
  R. 'Madame Isaac Pereire', 50, 59; *53, 57, 60, 62*
  R. 'National Trust', 93; *93*
  R. 'Nozomi', 90; *90*
  R. 'Paul Crampel', 16; *17*
  R. 'Pink Parfait', 82; *84, 88, 90*
  R. 'Sweet Fairy', 92; *92*
rose gardens, 82–93
  with dwarf shrubs, 90–1
  fragrant, 92
  with ground cover plants, 88–9
  ingredients, 82
  maintenance, 83–7
  planting, 83, 85
  tall, 92
Rosmarinus officinalis, 115; *116*
  R.o. 'Jessop's Upright', 22, 46, 79, 118, 123; *21; 47, 80, 121, 128, 129*

Rosemary *see Rosmarinus officinalis*
Rudbeckia fulgida 'Deamii', 26; *28, 36, 37*
  R. hirta 'Rustic Dwarfs', 137; *138*
rue *see Ruta graveolens*
Rumex scutatus, 46; *47*
ruta graveolens, 16; *17*
  R.g. 'Jackman's Blue', 44, 46; *45, 47*

S
sage *see Salvia officinalis*
St John's wort *see Hypericum*
Salvia officinalis, 38, 43, 44, 46, 48; *40, 43, 45, 47, 48*
  S.o. 'Purpurea', 22, 79, 90, 123; *24, 80, 124*
  S.o. 'Tricolor', 46; *47*
  S. × superba, 31, 35; *32, 36*
Sambucus canadensis 'Aurea', 123; *124*
  S. racemosa 'Plumosa Aurea', 18, 22, 160; *19, 24, 163, 167, 169*
Santolina chamaecyparissus, 66, 90, 118; *68, 76, 78, 80, 90, 121*
sawara cypress *see Chamaecyparis pisifera*
Saxifraga moschata 'Cloth of Gold', 125; *126*
  S. × urbium, 59, 66; *60, 68, 74, 78*
Scabious *see Scabiosa*
Scabiosa caucasica 'Clive Greaves', 61, 125; *62, 126*
scented plants:
  old-fashioned borders, 56–8
  shrub borders, 115–16
Scilla sibirica, 77; *78*
Scirpus tabernaemontani 'Zebrinus', 144; *146, 155, 156*
sedge *see Carex*
Sedum 'Autumn Joy', 16, 26, 73; *17, 24, 28, 36, 37, 74*
Sempervivum, 73; *74*
Senecio laxifolius, 8; *11, 17, 24*
  S. 'Sunshine', 118; *121, 129*
shady borders:
  dry, 125–6
  mixed planting, 18–19
  old-fashioned borders, 63–5
shasta daisy *see Chrysanthemum maximum*
shrub borders, 104–15
  foliage effect, 111–12
  fragrant, 115–16
  ingredients, 104
  long, 109–10
  maintenance, 107–8
  planting, 107

year-round colour, 113–14
Silene dioica, 170; *171*
silver fir *see Abies koreana*
snapdragon *see Antirrhinum*
snowdrop *see Galanthus nivalis*
Solidago caesia, 63; *65*
  S. 'Golden Sun', 26
Solomon's seal *see Polygonatum*
  multiflorum
spearmint *see Mentha spicata*
spindle tree *see Euonymus*
Spiraea × bumalda 'Anthony
  Waterer', 113, 125; *114, 126*
  S. × b. 'Gold Flame', 104; *106, 110*
Stachys lanata, 22, 33, 35, 142; *24, 34,*
  36, 143
Stellaria holostea, 170; *171*
stinking hellebores *see Helleborus*
  foetidus
summer borders, 132–43
  colour contrast, 137–8
  colour harmony, 138–9
  for foliage, 140–1
  ingredients, 132
  maintenance, 134–6
  perennials, 142–3
  planting, 134–5
summer cypress *see Kochia*
  trichophylla
summer hyacinth *see Galtonia*
  candicans
sweet bay *see Laurus nobilis*
sweet cicely *see Myrrhis odorata*
sweet marjoram *see Origanum*
  majorana
sweet peas *see lathyrus odorata*
sweet rocket *see Hesperis*
  matronalis

T
Tagetes erecta 'Gold Galore', 137; *138*
  T. 'Naughty Maria', 137; *138*
  T. patula, 8; *11*
  T.p. 'Suzy Wong', 129; *129*
threadleaf coreopsis *see Coreopsis*
  verticilliata
Thrift *see Armeria maritima*
Thuja occidentalis 'Rheingold', 99; *97*
  T. orientalis 'Aurea Nana', 94, 99,
    101; *97, 99, 101*
Thyme *see Thymus vulgaris*
Thyme vulgaris 38, 43, 46, 48; *40, 43,*
  47, 48
tobacco plant *see Nicotiana alata*
torch lily *see Kniphofia*
Tropaeolum majus 'Climbing Mixed',
  46, 140; *47, 141*
Tsuga canadensis 'Pendula', 100; *100*
Tulipa fosteriana 'Cantata', 77
Typha minima, 144; *146, 150, 155,*
  156

V
Valeriana officinalis, 150; *150*
Verbascum bombyciferum 'Silver
  Lining', 50; *53, 60*
Viburnum fragrans, 115; *116*
  V. rhytidophyllum, 168; *169*
  V. tinus, 104, 113; *106, 110, 114*
Viola riviniana, 170; *171*
  V. 'Swiss Giants', 63
  V. 'Violet Queen', 56; *57*
  V. 'Yellow Queen', 61; *62*
Virginian stock *see Malcolmia*
  maritima

W
walls, beds bordering, 37–8
water crowfoot *see Ranunculus*
  aquatilis
water forget-me-not *see Myosotis*
  alpestris
water gardens, 144–58
  boggy banks, 153–5
  circular ponds, 156
  fish ponds, 157–8
  ingredients, 144
  maintenance, 147–9
  planting, 147–9
  wildlife ponds, 150–2
water hawthorn *see Aponogeton*
  distachyon
water lily *see Nymphaea*
water violet *see Hottonia palustris*
Weigela florida 'Foliis Purpureis', 109;
  110
wildflowers, woodland clearing, 170–
  1
windflower *see Anemone blanda*
woodland gardens, 160–71
  acid soil, 165–6
  alkaline soil, 167
  damp soil, 168
  ingredients, 160
  maintenance, 162–4
  planting, 162–4
  wildflower clearing, 170–1

Y
yarrow *see Achillea*
yellow archangel *see Lamium*
  galeobdolon
Yucca filamentosa, 73, 127; *74,*
  128

Printed in Italy - by Milanostampa Farigliano (CN)